52 Weeks of Recipes

for Students, Missionaries, and Nervous Cooks

Clark L. & Kathryn H. Kidd

DESERET
BOOK

Salt Lake City, Utah

To Shauna Dickson, Susie Wiedeman, and Barbara Covey,
for recipes and friendship

Library of Congress Cataloging-in-Publication Data

Kidd, Clark.
    52 weeks of recipes for students, missionaries, and nervous cooks / Clark L. Kidd and Kathryn H. Kidd.
        p. cm.
    Includes index.
    ISBN-13: 978-1-59038-792-4 (pbk.)
    1. Cookery, American. I. Kidd, Kathy H. II. Title. III. Title: Fifty-two weeks of recipes for students, missionaries, and nervous cooks.
    TX715.K426 2007
    641.5973—dc22   2007019194

Printed in the United States of America
R. R. Donnelley and Sons, Crawfordsville, IN

10   9   8   7   6   5   4   3   2   1

Contents

How to Use This Book

WE DESIGNED THIS BOOK TO BE USEFUL to all cooks—from novices who get weak knees at the prospect of having to boil water to experts who can whip up a nine-course meal without breaking a sweat.

Experienced cooks should be able to find easy recipes here for those days when they're just too tired to prepare elaborate meals or when they don't feel like driving to the store for some exotic ingredient. Just because these recipes are easy doesn't mean the food will not be tasty, nutritious (well, most of the time), and easy on the budget.

But our real focus is those readers who are just beginning to learn to cook for themselves. This book is ideal for people who are away from home for the first time on an extended basis—students, missionaries, young people just starting a new career in a new city. If you're one of these people, you've probably already realized that cooking is not always easy. How did Mom and Dad manage all of those pots so that everything would arrive at the table at the same time?

After a few failed attempts, you might have decided to leave the cooking to others. Maybe your freezer is full of packaged foods that are only a few microwave minutes from the table. Or maybe it's just easier to make a detour through the closest fast-food outlet on your way home. Although a constant diet of pizza and burgers may sound appealing at first, it can also be expensive, unhealthy, and a little boring on the palate. And when the time comes for you to think of finding the right person to marry, your prospective spouse will be a lot more impressed if you can put together a good meal than if you simply know the best place in town to get a good pizza.

If you are currently on a first-name basis with the order-takers at all the local fast food outlets, then this is the book for you. You will find recipes for each week of the year, and the recipes we'll offer will be easy and usually inexpensive. Some weeks we have provided recipes that could be a complete meal—an entree and a side dish or dessert—if you are feeling brave enough to tackle two new recipes in one night, but most of the recipes are designed to supplement your current collection of favorite foods. If you're *really* a beginner, they can even be used as the starting point in your cooking career. You can go through the book week by week, or you may choose to jump around and find something that sounds appealing. Use the comprehensive index at the end of the book to find recipes by subject (desserts, main dishes, and so on) or by ingredient (ground beef, chicken, and so on).

One common cookbook mistake is to assume that a reader will understand a specific cooking term or a cooking procedure. This can be frustrating if you don't know the difference between basting, boiling, and broiling, or if you don't already know how to cook pasta or boil an egg. We have tried to avoid these problems by describing common cooking procedures in Appendix A and defining common cooking terms and ingredients in Appendix B. If a recipe includes a term or ingredient you've never heard of, you'll find it described in Appendix B. Appendix C will show you what equipment you absolutely need to have if you're cooking—and we'll throw in four basic seasoning mixes that will turn your recipes into works of art.

We also simplified the directions by listing all the temperatures in the book on the Fahrenheit scale.

Not every recipe will appeal to every reader, so we have included a rating system with every recipe. After you try each one, you can rate it from one star (No Way!) to five stars (Great!). Feel free to add other ingredients or to experiment with the recipes in other ways. If you like the results, you can document your changes for future reference. Jot down your notes right in the book—in the margins, next to the ingredients list, or wherever you want. Recipes should be personalized, so write down what works for you (and what doesn't!).

One phrase that professional chefs often use is "Cooking is an art, but baking is a science." So although you can't change proportions of ingredients in a cake or pastry without ruining the recipe, you can do all sorts of adjustments to recipes if you aren't baking. If you only have one tomato and the recipe calls for three, or if the recipe specifies a 16-ounce can of chili and all you can find is 14.5 ounces, *the world will not end!* And if the recipe calls for you to sprinkle an ounce of cheese on your salad but you want to use a cup of it, there are no recipe police who will haul you off to jail. *This is a no-stress cookbook. You are forbidden to get stressed out about it!*

Happy cooking!

Week 1

This week's recipes make a nice dinner for two to serve on a cold night. Add salad to the mix and you'll have a complete meal; or serve the soup with sandwiches for a delicious light meal. These recipes might be your first exposure to cooking rice. If you want to cook it separately, instructions for cooking rice—and pasta, too—can be found in Appendix A.

Chicken and Rice ☆☆☆☆☆

½ cup long-grain rice, brown or white (do not use instant!)
1 cup water
1 (10.75-ounce) can cream of chicken soup
1 (1-ounce) package dry onion soup mix
2 boneless, skinless chicken breasts

PREHEAT OVEN TO 325 DEGREES. Combine rice, water, soup, and soup mix and pour into an 8x8-inch baking dish. Top with chicken breasts. Cover with aluminum foil. Bake two hours.

Serves 2.

Tomato Pasta Soup ☆☆☆☆☆

2 tablespoons vegetable oil
1 cup diced onion
1 teaspoon minced garlic
1 teaspoon dried oregano
1 cup diced green pepper (optional)
1 cup diced zucchini (optional)
1 (14.5-ounce) can diced tomatoes, including juice
1 (14-ounce) can chicken broth
1 cup dry pasta (any shape will do, but shells are good)
  Grated cheese, for topping

HEAT THE OIL IN A LARGE SAUCEPAN over low heat; add onion and cook until no longer crunchy, about 5 to 7 minutes. Stir in garlic and oregano. (See Appendix A for directions on mincing garlic.) Add green pepper and zucchini, if using. Stir in tomatoes, broth, and pasta. Increase heat to high and bring mixture to a boil. Cover pan, reduce heat to low, and cook for 7 minutes or until pasta is tender. Serve topped with grated cheese.

Serves 2.

Week 2

If it's a cold winter night, you want something that will stick to your ribs. This week's recipes are so easy that anyone can make them. Remember—most of the measurements and ingredients in the first recipe can be varied according to your taste. If you want to add more cheese or use less macaroni, or if you want to make your meal spicier by adding some sliced jalapenos, go right ahead and experiment! Be sure to refrigerate the leftovers so you can warm them up for tomorrow's supper (or breakfast!). The second recipe is a great starter for a meal or a good way to get warm on a chilly day.

Beefy Mac and Cheese ☆☆☆☆☆

1   pound lean ground beef (you can also use ground chicken
       or turkey)
1   onion, chopped
     Salt, to taste
     Garlic powder, to taste
1   (16-ounce) package small, shaped pasta or elbow macaroni,
       cooked according to package directions
1   (14.5-ounce) can diced tomatoes, drained
1   cup sour cream (optional)
1 to 2 cups shredded cheddar cheese

PREHEAT THE OVEN TO 350 DEGREES. Place the meat and the onion in a frying pan and brown over medium-high heat, seasoning with salt and garlic powder, to taste. Drain the macaroni and add it to the meat mixture, along with the tomatoes, the sour cream (if using), and most of the cheese. Stir well. Put the mixture in a 2-quart baking dish. Sprinkle more cheese on top if you want to. Bake for 30 minutes.

See Appendix A if you are unsure about how to cook pasta.

Serves 2 to 4, depending on whether or not you want leftovers.

Joy Lundberg's Miracle Clam Chowder ☆☆☆☆☆

2	(6.5-ounce) cans minced clams, undrained
1	cup finely chopped onion
1	cup finely chopped celery
2	cups finely chopped potatoes
¾	cup (1½ sticks) butter
¾	cup flour
1	quart half-and-half
1½	teaspoons salt
	Dash of black pepper
½	teaspoon sugar

DRAIN THE JUICE FROM THE CLAMS and reserve. Place chopped vegetables in a medium saucepan and cover with reserved clam juice; add enough water to the saucepan to barely cover the vegetables. Simmer, covered, over medium heat until vegetables are soft. While the vegetables simmer, melt the butter in a second saucepan over medium-high heat; add flour and blend well, cooking for a minute or two, until the mixture is a nutty brown color. Add the half-and-half and cook and stir until smooth and thick, using a wire whisk (or a fork, if you don't have a wire whisk) to blend. Watch and stir this carefully because it burns easily. Add the vegetables, along with the liquid they cooked in. Finally, stir in the clams and heat through. Season the mixture with salt, pepper, and sugar.

Serves 8.

Fruit Cocktail Cake ☆☆☆☆☆

- 1   (16-ounce) can fruit cocktail
- 1   cup flour
- 1   cup white sugar
- ½   teaspoon salt
- 1   teaspoon baking powder
- 1   egg
- ½   cup brown sugar

PREHEAT THE OVEN TO 325 DEGREES. Spray a square baking dish with cooking spray, or coat it lightly with butter or vegetable oil, then set it aside. Pour the fruit cocktail (including the juice) into a medium-sized bowl. Add in the flour, white sugar, salt, baking powder, and egg. Stir the mixture until it is just combined and then pour it into the prepared pan. Sprinkle the top with the brown sugar. Bake the cake for 45 minutes or until the top is golden brown.

Serves 9.

Week 3

Salmon is so healthy for you that many nutritionists recommend eating it at least twice a week. Fortunately, salmon is also easy to make. Here's a recipe for baked salmon, along with one for potatoes that taste just as good (but probably shouldn't be eaten twice a week). You can use any leftover salmon later in the week to top a salad.

Baked Salmon ☆☆☆☆☆

4   (6-ounce) salmon fillets, cut ½- to 1-inch thick
1   teaspoon seasoning salt
     Dried oregano (optional)
     Black pepper (optional)
4   teaspoons butter
     Lemon (optional)

YOU'LL NEED TO BUY SALMON FILLETS (pronounced fill-LAYS) from the fish or meat counter at your local market. Just ask for pieces that are about 6 ounces in weight and ½- to 1-inch thick, which is an average serving size. Many markets sell salmon that is already cleaned, ready to cook, and cut into serving-sized pieces. If the salmon is more than you want to eat, either cut off what you want before cooking, or cook the entire piece and refrigerate the leftovers.

Preheat the oven to 450 degrees. Spray a shallow 9x13-inch baking dish with cooking spray, or rub it with butter. Arrange the salmon fillets in the dish so that the sides aren't touching each other or the dish. Sprinkle each fillet with ¼ teaspoon of the seasoning salt. If you want to add pepper or sprinkle on some oregano, now is the time (put on as much or little as your taste dictates)! Put a teaspoon of butter (a teaspoon of butter is about the size of a grape, if you don't want to measure) on top of each fillet. Bake 8 to 10 minutes (about 5 minutes for every ½ inch of thickness). When the fish is done, it will be light pink rather than red in the middle and it will flake easily with a fork.

Serves 4.

Mashed Potatoes ☆☆☆☆☆

1½	pounds red or white or gold potatoes (brown ones are for baking)
1	tablespoon salt
4	tablespoons (½ stick) butter
⅓ to ½	cup milk
	Salt, to taste
	Black pepper, to taste

PEEL THE POTATOES, unless you like mashed potatoes with the skins on. (If you like mashed potatoes with the skins on, scrub them like crazy with a vegetable scrubber before you cook them.) Cut the potatoes into pieces about 1-inch thick (make them the same size so they will take the same amount of time to cook). Put the potatoes in a large pot (3-quart saucepan) and pour in enough water to just cover them. (Leave plenty of space at the top of the pot so that the water won't boil over!) Add the tablespoon salt.

Cook over medium-high heat until the potato pieces don't offer any resistance when stabbed with a fork, this is about 10 to 15 minutes. Drain immediately, then put the potatoes in a large mixing bowl. Add the butter and about ⅓ cup of the milk. Mix on high speed with an electric mixer to get the lumps out, adding small amounts of additional milk, or even some extra butter, to get the consistency you like. (If you don't have an electric mixer, you can buy an inexpensive potato masher at the supermarket and mash the potatoes by hand.) Add salt and pepper to taste. If you don't serve immediately, put aluminum foil over the mixing bowl to keep the potatoes hot until ready to serve.

As a variation, boil a peeled carrot or two with the potatoes and mash them in. Nobody will know exactly what it is you've put in the potatoes, but the mashed potatoes will taste terrific.

Serves 4.

Green Jell-O Fluff ☆☆☆☆☆

1 (12-ounce) carton cottage cheese
1 (16-ounce) tub of Cool Whip, thawed
1 (8-ounce) can crushed pineapple, drained
1 (3-ounce) package lime Jell-O® or instant pistachio pudding

MIX ALL THE INGREDIENTS in a bowl until combined well. Feel free to add optional ingredients such as 1 cup of miniature marshmallows, ½ cup maraschino cherries, or even ½ cup of chopped pecans. Pour in a glass baking dish and chill until ready to serve.

Serves 6 to 10.

Week 4

This first recipe is perfect for a quick salad that can round out almost any meal. The other recipe is a slightly upgraded version of the classic tuna casserole.

Lettuce Wedge Salad ☆☆☆☆☆

1   head iceberg lettuce
1   tomato, chopped
1   bunch green onions and tops, chopped (optional)
1   bottle bleu cheese dressing (look for it in the refrigerator
      case near the lettuce)
      Crumbled bleu cheese (look for it in the cheese case of the
      grocery store—optional)

SALAD DOESN'T GET ANY EASIER THAN THIS. Wash the lettuce and cut out the core from the bottom of the head. Don't cut yourself! Cut the lettuce into six wedges. Put each wedge on a salad plate so that the pointed side is sticking up. Sprinkle chopped tomato and green onions over the wedge. Pour a little bleu cheese dressing over the lettuce and sprinkle the bleu cheese on top.

Serves 6.

Tuna Noodles Romanoff ☆☆☆☆☆

4	cups uncooked egg noodles
2	cans tuna, well drained
1½	cups sour cream
¾	cup milk
1	(3-ounce) can sliced mushrooms, drained
1½	teaspoons salt
¼	teaspoon black pepper
¼	cup dry bread crumbs
¼	cup grated Parmesan cheese
2	tablespoons butter, melted
	Paprika

PREHEAT OVEN TO 350 DEGREES. Cook and drain the noodles. (If you don't know how to cook noodles/pasta, see Appendix A.) Mix the noodles, tuna, sour cream, milk, mushrooms, salt, and pepper in an ungreased casserole dish. Combine bread crumbs, Parmesan cheese, and butter in a small bowl. Sprinkle cheese-crumb mixture over casserole, then sprinkle with paprika. Heat the mixture for 30 minutes, or until bubbly and heated through. Remove from the oven and let cool 5 minutes before serving.

Serves 4.

Week 5

No matter the reason you have friends coming in for a visit, chicken wings make a good addition to the menu. Here we have two recipes for chicken wings—buffalo wings and Chinese chicken wings. Either one will brighten up a party, or you can eat them as the main course, even if you're dining alone.

Buffalo Wings ☆☆☆☆☆

- 1 cup flour
- 1 teaspoon seasoning salt
- 1 teaspoon black pepper
- ⅛ teaspoon garlic powder
- 40 chicken wing pieces
- 1 cup Louisiana red hot sauce (Texas Pete® is a good brand)
- 1 tablespoon butter or margarine, melted
- Celery sticks (optional)
- 1 bottle bleu cheese salad dressing

MOST MARKETS SELL chicken wing pieces, which are portions of the chicken already cut into pieces—just the right size for making buffalo wings. Preheat oven to 425 degrees. Mix the flour, seasoning salt, pepper, and garlic powder in a large, zip-top storage bag. Add about six wing pieces at a time to the bag and shake to coat the pieces with flour. Place coated wings on the top part of a broiler pan (that's the two-piece pan you usually find in the bottom of an oven) or a cookie sheet and cook for one hour. Turn pieces over with a long fork half-way through cooking time.

While the chicken is cooking, combine melted butter and hot sauce in a medium bowl. After cooking, dip individual wings into the sauce mixture and then serve with celery sticks and bleu cheese dressing.

Serves 4 to 6.

Chinese Chicken Wings ☆☆☆☆☆

18	chicken wings
1	gallon-size zip-top storage bag
½	cup soy sauce
½	cup rice vinegar
¼	cup vegetable oil
4	cloves garlic, minced
1	tablespoon fresh grated ginger
2	teaspoons Chinese five spice powder

PREHEAT OVEN TO 425 DEGREES. Put wings in the plastic zip-top bag. Mix remaining ingredients in a medium-sized bowl and then add to the bag. Zip bag shut and refrigerate for at least an hour so the wings can marinate. Grease or spray the bottom of a rectangular glass baking dish. Place wings in the dish and cook for 45 minutes. Halfway through the cooking, turn over the wings and baste with leftover marinade before returning to the oven.

Serves 2 to 4.

Week 6

The festival of Mardi Gras—also called Carnival in some areas of the world—culminates on a Tuesday, forty-one days before Easter Sunday. Although most of us don't live in an area where Mardi Gras is celebrated, we can enjoy Louisiana food any time of the year. These recipes lend a New Orleans flavor without any of the old-fashioned work. Once you master them, you can consider yourself a Cajun cook.

Chicken or Shrimp Gumbo ☆☆☆☆☆

½	cup cooking oil
½	cup flour
1 to 2	(16-ounce) bags frozen okra
2	onions, chopped
1	(14.5-ounce) can diced tomatoes, undrained
3	(14-ounce) cans chicken broth
	Water
1	cooked rotisserie chicken, cut in pieces, or 2 pounds raw shrimp tails, with shells off
	Salt, to taste
	Black pepper, to taste
	Cayenne pepper, to taste
	Garlic powder, to taste
6	cups cooked rice

MAKE A DARK ROUX (often called a chocolate roux, because of its dark color) by heating the oil over low heat, then stirring in the flour until the mixture is smooth. Continue stirring until the roux turns a nice, fudgy brown color, about 12 to 15 minutes. (Be careful to keep stirring, so the mixture doesn't burn.) See Appendix A for more details on making a roux. Stir in the frozen okra and the chopped onions until the vegetables are coated with the roux. Add the can of tomatoes, along with its juice, and stir again. Add broth plus three soup cans of water. Now is the time to add the shrimp or chicken. If the shrimp are big, cut them into bite-sized pieces first. Add salt, black pepper, cayenne pepper, and garlic powder to taste. This is supposed to be spicy, so don't be afraid to use that cayenne pepper! Simmer, covered, for a couple of hours, stirring occasionally. Serve over rice.

Serves 8 to 12.

Botchie's Peach Salad ☆☆☆☆☆

- 1 (8-ounce) package cream cheese, softened
- 2 tablespoons Miracle Whip®
- ¼ cup minced celery (chop it very, very small!)
- ¼ cup chopped pecans
- 1 (15-ounce) can peach halves
  Lettuce leaves

BLEND THE CREAM CHEESE and the Miracle Whip with an electric mixer until smooth and combined well. Stir in the celery and pecans. Fill the centers of the canned peach halves with the cheese mixture and serve on lettuce leaves.

Serves 4 to 6.

Week 7

Sometimes you may want a festive dinner, but festive doesn't have to be difficult. Here's a recipe for easy beef stroganoff. If you want to try a variation, use chicken breasts instead. You'll have two recipes for the price of one!

Easy Beef Stroganoff ☆☆☆☆☆

8	ounces fresh mushrooms, sliced (typically found in the produce section in square cartons)
2	tablespoons cooking oil
1½	pounds stew beef (with fat trimmed off)
1	(16-ounce) package egg noodles
2	(10.75-ounce) cans cream of mushroom soup
1	cup sour cream

WASH THE MUSHROOMS BY SOAKING THEM in cold water for a minute; drain well. Heat oil in a frying pan or 12-inch skillet over medium-high heat. Add beef and mushrooms and cook until the meat is nicely browned. Stir so the mushrooms don't burn! Stir in soup and sour cream. Continue cooking until all ingredients are hot and the soup is no longer lumpy. If you can make this ahead of time, it tastes better when you refrigerate the meat mixture for a day before eating. (Don't forget to reheat it if you do this.) Whether you wait or eat right away, prepare the noodles according to package directions shortly before you are ready to serve the dish. Drain noodles and put them in a serving bowl. Pour the beef mixture on top. See Appendix A for instructions on making perfect pasta.

Serves 4 to 6.

Dump Cake ☆☆☆☆☆

1   package yellow cake mix
1   (20-ounce) can crushed pineapple, undrained
1   (20-ounce) can pie filling (any flavor)
¾   cup (1½ sticks) butter, melted

PREHEAT OVEN TO 350 DEGREES. Dump all ingredients, in the order listed, into a 9x13-inch glass baking dish and bake until the top is browned nicely, approximately 1 hour. This tastes good when served with ice cream or whipped cream.

Serves 12.

Week 8

Maybe you are brimming with energy today, or maybe you've got a little aggression you'd like to release. If you're looking for a way to release your energy or vent your frustration, there's nothing like pounding a chicken breast as flat as the proverbial pancake. In the process, you can make yourself some terrific comfort food.

Fried Chicken and Gravy ☆☆☆☆☆

    1   cup plus 6 tablespoons flour
    1   teaspoon salt
    1   teaspoon garlic powder
    2   teaspoons paprika
        Black pepper, to taste
    2   eggs, beaten
   3½   cups milk, divided (that means you won't use it all at once
          in this recipe)
    6   boneless, skinless chicken breasts
        Vegetable oil
    1   tablespoon butter

COMBINE 1 CUP OF THE FLOUR with the salt, garlic powder, paprika, and pepper on a plate or in a gallon-sized, zipper-top plastic storage bag; set aside. In a shallow bowl, combine beaten eggs and ½ cup of the milk; set aside. Spread plastic wrap on top of the counter or a large cutting board. Place chicken on the plastic wrap and top with another piece of plastic. Pound each piece of chicken until it's as flat as you can get it. (There are meat mallets made for this purpose in any store that sells cooking supplies, or you can improvise with any *clean* kitchen tool that won't put a hole in your kitchen counter or break your cutting board to smithereens.) Dip each chicken breast in the milk mixture, then coat with flour mixture by dredging on the plate or shaking in the bag.

Pour vegetable oil a quarter-inch deep in a heavy frying pan and heat over medium heat. The oil will be hot enough if it sizzles when a drop of water is added to the pan. Place the chicken in the pan and cook until browned on one side; turn over to cook on the other side. Once browned, remove chicken and drain off grease on a paper towel. Add butter to the drippings in the pan and mix until the butter is melted. Stir in the 6 tablespoons flour and cook and stir over medium heat until the flour browns, about 5 minutes. Add 3 cups milk and stir over medium heat until mixture is thickened. Season with salt and pepper and pour over warm chicken. Serve with mashed potatoes.

Serves 6.

Sugar Beans ☆☆☆☆☆

1	(14.5-ounce) can cut green beans, with liquid
1 to 2	strips bacon
	Garlic powder, to taste
½	of a large onion, diced
2	tablespoons sugar
	Salt, to taste
	Black pepper, to taste

POUR THE BEANS, LIQUID AND ALL, into a medium saucepan. Cut the bacon into bits and add them to the saucepan. Add several healthy shakes of garlic powder. Add the remaining ingredients and cook over medium heat, stirring occasionally, long enough for the onions to turn translucent and the bacon to cook. The bacon will never get brown, but the fat will soak out of it and flavor the beans. If you want to pick the bacon pieces out afterwards, that's fine as long as the bacon has cooked long enough to lend its flavor to the beans. When they're done, the beans should have a garlic flavor and be sweet. Drain off excess liquid before serving.

Serves 2.

Week 9

If you've never cooked grilled cheese sandwiches, now is your chance. They're so easy you'll be a pro after your first sandwich. Finish off the meal with an easy fruit cobbler, and you'll think it's a miracle that you put together such a fine meal as a novice cook.

Grilled Cheese Sandwiches ☆☆☆☆☆

2   slices bread
    Butter
2   slices (about 1½ ounces) cheese, any kind—cheddar, Swiss, Monterey Jack, American)

GRILLED CHEESE SANDWICHES may not be health food, but they're easy to fix. All you need are the above ingredients, a frying pan, and a spatula.

First, butter one side of each slice of bread. Place cheese on the buttered side of one of the slices of bread. Top cheese with remaining bread slice, making sure the buttered side faces down.

Butter the top side of sandwich, and place it, butter-side down, in a frying pan. Having butter on the outside of the sandwich is what gives it that nice grilled texture and flavor.

Turn the heat to medium-low (any higher and the sandwich will burn before the cheese melts). Use a spatula to press down on the sandwich, so that it gets nice and flat and the ingredients melt together. After you have pressed down the sandwich, spread butter on the side of the sandwich that is facing up in the pan. This means that, eventually, both sides of both pieces of bread will be buttered.

Use the spatula to lift the sandwich occasionally and check the bottom. When it is a golden brown, turn it over and brown it on the other side as well. You can turn the sandwich several times during cooking, if needed, and continue to press it down with the spatula. As soon as the sandwich is pleasantly browned on both sides and the cheese is melted, dinner is served. If the bread is as brown as you want it to get and the cheese still isn't melted, pop the sandwich in the microwave for 5 seconds or so.

Makes 1 sandwich. Allow 1 to 2 sandwiches for each person being served.

Three-Minute Cobbler ☆☆☆☆☆

- ½ cup (1 stick) butter
- 1 cup flour
- 2 teaspoons baking powder
- ¾ cup milk
- ¼ teaspoon salt
- 1 (15-ounce) can fruit, drained, or 1 (21-ounce) can fruit pie filling

PREHEAT OVEN TO 350 DEGREES. Melt butter in a 1-quart, square, baking dish in the microwave. Add flour, sugar, baking powder, milk, and salt. Stir to combine (this will remove most of the lumps, but mixture will still be lumpy). Drain fruit and pour on top of the flour mixture. Do not stir! Bake until brown on top, about 50 minutes. This dessert is great with ice cream or whipped cream.

Serves 4.

Week 10

Almost everybody likes spaghetti, and it's easier to eat when it's in the form of a casserole. This is something that's easy to cook and that can become a family favorite. Don't forget the garlic (or Parmesan) bread!

Spaghetti Casserole ☆☆☆☆☆

- 1   pound dry spaghetti
- 1   pound lean ground beef, browned, and drained
- 2   cups shredded cheddar cheese
- 3   (14.5-ounce) cans stewed tomatoes, with most of the liquid drained off

PREHEAT OVEN TO 350 DEGREES. Cook spaghetti in 4 quarts boiling, salted water until tender; drain. Combine spaghetti and remaining ingredients in a large baking dish. Bake, uncovered, for 1 hour.

Once you've made this, you can tailor it to your own tastes. Make it spicier with cayenne pepper, or add sliced and drained black (or green) olives to the casserole. Garlic would also be a great addition. You can even add cooked meatballs. Be creative!

See Appendix A for more hints on cooking pasta and browning ground beef.

Serves 4.

Garlic Bread / Parmesan Bread ☆☆☆☆☆

- 1   baguette or loaf French bread
      Butter, softened

Garlic powder or grated Parmesan cheese
Seasoning salt (optional)

SLICE YOUR BAGUETTE EITHER IN HALF LENGTHWISE or in inch-wide slices from top to bottom. If you slice the baguette from top to bottom, slice the bread *almost* all the way through, so the bread stays in one loaf but the pieces will be easy to tear off.

If your bread is sliced lengthwise, spread softened butter on each half and then sprinkle a little garlic powder on top. (With Parmesan bread, omit the garlic powder and use Parmesan cheese instead.) Place the loaf, buttered sides up, under the broiler until the butter melts and the bread is just starting to turn brown.

If your bread is sliced from top to bottom, melt the butter in a saucepan, stir in the garlic powder or Parmesan cheese, and pour the mixture between the cuts in the sliced bread so that every piece of bread has a little butter on it. Place the loaf of bread in the middle of the oven and bake at 400 degrees for about five minutes, until the bread is warm.

If you want to add a gourmet touch to your garlic bread, melt a stick of butter in a saucepan over low heat and add a crushed garlic clove or two! Pour the garlic butter on the bread halves or between the sliced cuts of the whole loaf and cook as already described. The pressed garlic has a much better taste than garlic powder, although pressing is a little more trouble than just shaking powder out of the garlic container.

Serves 4 to 6.

Week 11

There's an old saying that everyone is Irish on St. Patrick's Day. Here are some Irish recipes to commemorate the season. The stew is probably Irish in name only, but the Easy Irish Soda Bread would satisfy even a Leprechaun. If you ever wanted to make bread but were afraid of using yeast, here is how the Irish do it.

Huff Mulligan Stew ☆☆☆☆☆

1   pound ground beef
1   medium onion, chopped
1   cup uncooked elbow macaroni
1   (1.25-ounce) package chili seasoning
1   (14.5-ounce) can diced tomatoes, undrained
1   (15.5-ounce) can kidney beans, drained

COOK THE BEEF AND THE ONION in a large skillet over medium-high heat until the beef is no longer pink. Drain off fat if necessary. Cook macaroni according to package directions, and drain. (See Appendix A if you are unsure about cooking pasta.) Add macaroni to beef mixture. Blend in chili seasoning and tomatoes. Cover and simmer over medium-low heat for 5 minutes or until everything is hot. Stir in beans and heat through.

Serves 2 to 4.

Irish Soda Bread ☆☆☆☆☆

4   cups flour

4   tablespoons sugar

1   teaspoon baking soda

1   tablespoon baking powder

½   teaspoon salt

½   cup (1 stick) butter, softened

1¼ cup buttermilk, divided

1   egg, beaten

¼   cup (½ stick) butter, melted

PREHEAT OVEN TO 375 DEGREES. Lightly grease a large cookie sheet and set aside.

In a large bowl, combine flour, sugar, baking soda, baking powder, salt, and the ½ cup softened butter. Stir in 1 cup of the buttermilk and the egg. Put dough on a clean, flat surface that has been lightly dusted with flour. Work the dough with your hands for a minute or two, flattening the dough then folding it over and pressing it down again with the heel of your hand (12 to 14 turns will do). After working the dough, form it into a circle about 6 inches in diameter and 2 or 2½ inches high and place on prepared baking sheet. In a small bowl, combine the ¼ cup melted butter with the remaining ¼ cup buttermilk. Brush the top and sides of the loaf with the buttermilk-butter mix. Use a sharp knife to cut an 'X' in the top of the loaf.

Bake 45 to 50 minutes, or until a toothpick inserted into the center of the loaf comes out clean. You may continue to brush the loaf with the butter mixture while it bakes.

Serves 4 to 6.

Week 12

If you ever wanted an easy meal, ham steak is about as easy as it gets. If you're not sure what a ham steak is, it's just a slice of ham that's about one-quarter to three-quarters of an inch thick. It usually has the bone in the middle. If you can't find it at your supermarket, anyone at the meat counter can help you. Ham steaks are generally pre-cooked, so all you have to do is warm them and eat.

Ham Steak ☆☆☆☆☆

- 1   ham steak
- 1   tablespoon brown sugar
- 1   teaspoon prepared mustard

PREHEAT OVEN TO 350 DEGREES. Put the ham steak in a shallow baking dish. Cover the dish with aluminum foil and bake for 10 minutes. Pour the juices that cooked out of the ham into a small bowl and stir in the brown sugar and mustard. Spread the juice mixture over the top of the ham and cook for 3 minutes longer. Remove from oven, cover with aluminum foil, and let stand for a few minutes before serving.

Serves 1 to 2.

Green Beans Deluxe ☆☆☆☆☆

- ½   cup (1 stick) butter (don't even think about using margarine or whipped butter)
- 2   (14.5-ounce) cans cut green beans, drained

Garlic powder, to taste

½   cup freshly grated Parmesan cheese

Seasoning salt, to taste

MELT BUTTER IN A MEDIUM SAUCEPAN over medium heat. Add the beans to the saucepan. Sprinkle heavily with garlic powder and most of the grated Parmesan cheese. Add seasoning salt according to your taste. Cook, stirring occasionally until the beans start getting soggy and begin falling apart. The Parmesan cheese will be stringy. Top with the remaining Parmesan cheese and serve.

Although canned green beans have little nutritive value (and these are particularly bad for you because of all the butter and cheese), they taste good enough that you'll want to eat them in mass quantities. Double the recipe if you're serving guests.

Serves 4.

Garlic Potatoes ☆☆☆☆☆

6   medium-sized red or white potatoes

Seasoning salt

Garlic powder

1   cup heavy cream

PREHEAT OVEN TO 350 DEGREES. Peel the potatoes and cut them into thin slices. Place the potatoes in a baking dish in layers, sprinkling some garlic powder and a little seasoning salt on top of each layer. Pour cream over the top of the completed dish and bake for an hour or so until the potatoes are cooked through and the tops are golden brown.

Serves 4.

Week 13

Any professional chef would tell you that the words "gourmet" and "tuna and noodles" do not belong within a mile of one another. But if you were a professional chef, you wouldn't need this book! Here's the best recipe for tuna and noodles you're ever likely to find. It's easy to make, and it's good enough to impress your friends. The Sage Chicken is also easy to make, but it makes a wonderful main course that should impress even the most discriminating dinner guests.

Gourmet Tuna and Noodles ☆☆☆☆☆

2   (6-ounce) cans white albacore tuna
2   tablespoons butter
1   tablespoon lemon juice
¼   teaspoon cayenne pepper
2   tablespoons dried parsley flakes
½   cup canned chicken broth
2   tablespoons capers, drained
1   cup heavy cream
1   (16-ounce) package cooked egg noodles or other pasta
    Freshly grated parmesan cheese, for topping (optional)
    Freshly ground black pepper, for topping (optional)
    Lemon wedges, for topping (optional)

CAPERS ARE A WONDERFUL INGREDIENT, even though they aren't something many beginning cooks keep in the kitchen. But if you really don't like the idea of capers, or you don't have any available, just throw in a cup or so of thawed frozen peas just before you're ready to serve this dish. Frozen peas are cooked before being frozen, so they can be added to many recipes without cooking and with just a little bit of thawing.

Drain the flaked tuna and sauté it in butter over medium heat until hot. Stir in lemon juice, cayenne pepper, parsley flakes, chicken broth, and capers and heat thoroughly. Add cream and heat thoroughly, making sure the mixture doesn't reach a boil. Serve over pasta, topped with freshly grated Parmesan cheese and freshly ground pepper and lemon wedges.

Serves 4 to 6.

Sage Chicken ☆☆☆☆☆

1 or 2   cut-up chickens (typically found in the meat section and labeled "whole, cut-up fryer")
   2   tablespoons vegetable oil
   2   (10.75-ounce) cans cream of mushroom soup
      Water
   1   tablespoon dried sage
      Salt, to taste
      Black pepper, to taste
   1   (16-ounce) package noodles, or 4 cups cooked rice

HEAT ONE TABLESPOON OIL in a large pot over medium-high heat; add half the chicken pieces and brown on both sides. Remove chicken to a bowl and add remaining oil to the pot. Heat oil, then add remaining chicken pieces. Once browned, return first batch of chicken to the pot. Add the soup, plus three-fourths of a soup can of water (you don't need to use exact measurements with this recipe!). Add the dried sage, plus salt and pepper to taste. Stir the mixture well to break up the soup and to make a smooth gravy. Cook over medium heat until the chicken is cooked through; stir occasionally to prevent the chicken from sticking to the pot. Add water if you want the gravy to be thinner. Serve the chicken and gravy over the cooked noodles or rice.

See Appendix A for instructions on making perfect rice and noodles.

Serves 2 to 4.

Parmesan Popovers ☆☆☆☆☆

1   cup flour
½   teaspoon salt
½   cup grated Parmesan cheese
2   eggs
1   cup milk

PREHEAT OVEN TO 450 DEGREES. In a medium-sized mixing bowl, combine the flour, salt and Parmesan cheese. In a second bowl, beat the eggs and milk, using a wire whisk or electric mixer; mix until fluffy. Fold the wet mixture into the dry mixture, and thoroughly combine. Coat a 6-cup muffin or popover panwith cooking spray. Divide the batter between the 6 cups. Bake for 15 minutes. Reduce heat to 350 degrees and bake for another 20 minutes, until popovers are golden brown. Cool slightly, then turn popvers from the pan.

Serves 6.

Week 14

The beginning of April brings those long spring mornings when it's sunny out but sometimes still too cool to spend a lot of time outside. What better excuse to stay inside and cook yourself a nice warm breakfast? This week's recipes all involve the incredible, edible egg. If you want something as easy as a scrambled egg or as complicated as an omelet, look no further.

Scrambled Eggs ☆☆☆☆☆

Eggs (approximately 2 per person)
Water
Salt and pepper, to taste
Optional ingredients: cheese, jalapeños, raw or sautéed
    onions, raw or sautéed green peppers, diced tomatoes,
    smoked salmon, diced ham, crumbled bacon, black
    olives, or whatever else you like in your eggs
1 tablespoon butter or cooking oil

BREAK THE EGGS INTO A BOWL and add about a tablespoon of water for every two eggs. (A lot of people use milk, but the professionals use water because it tastes creamier. Go figure!) Use a spoon to remove any pieces of shell that may have fallen into the mixture. Beat the mixture well with a fork to blend the yolks and whites together. Add a little salt and pepper, along with whatever optional ingredients you want to add, and stir.

Put about a tablespoon butter or cooking oil in the bottom of a frying pan (or spray with cooking spray) and melt over medium heat. (Note: If you're doubling or tripling the recipe to serve more people, don't increase the amount of butter or oil, only the number of eggs and the water.) Add eggs and cook, stirring continually, until the eggs are done. Some people like their eggs more solid than liquid, so cook them to meet the tastes of your audience. Serve immediately.

Serves 1 per 2 eggs used.

Omelets in a Bag ☆☆☆☆☆

    2   large eggs
    1   tablespoon shredded cheese
    1   tablespoon each of any other ingredients you like in your
            omelet (crumbled bacon, diced ham, onion, sliced black
            olives, jalapenos)
    1   small, zipper-top freezer bag
         Salt and pepper, to taste

CRACK THE EGGS RIGHT INTO THE PLASTIC BAG. Add the other ingredients. Zip the bag shut and carefully knead it with your fingers to mix the ingredients. Open the bag just a bit to "burp" the air out. Re-seal. Bring a pot of water to a boil. Drop the sealed bag into the boiling water. Boil for 5 minutes. Carefully remove bag from the water. Open bag and roll the omelet onto a plate. This is great for large groups, because multiple omelets can be finished at the same time and everyone can eat together, especially if you have two pots of water going at one time. Make sure to use freezer bags because they are sturdy enough to be boiled without disintegrating.

Serves 1 per plastic bag.

Week 15

There's something about shrimp scampi that turns any dinner into a celebration. Serve it over rice or linguini, or serve it with a baguette to dip into the sauce.

Shrimp Scampi ☆☆☆☆☆

2   pounds large uncooked shrimp, peeled and deveined

    Seasoning salt, to taste

    Black pepper, to taste

    Paul Prudhomme's® Seafood Magic®, to taste (optional, but it sure tastes good)

1½   cups (3 sticks) butter, melted

3   tablespoons minced garlic

3   green onions, chopped

    Juice of one lemon

    2 teaspoons finely chopped flat-leaf (Italian) parsley leaves

    ¼ teaspoon Tabasco sauce (optional)

RINSE OFF THE SHRIMP in a colander. Peel each individual shrimp by removing all the hard shell portions. This may include the head, the body, and the tail. Only the soft portions of the shrimp should remain. Arrange shrimp on a paper-towel-lined plate. Place another paper towel on top and pat the shrimp dry. Sprinkle the shrimp with seasoning salt, pepper, and the Seafood Magic, if using.

Place the shrimp in a broiler-safe baking dish; set aside. Combine butter, garlic, onions, lemon, parsley, and Tabasco in a medium bowl and pour, by spoonfuls, over the shrimp. Broil for around 5 minutes, until the shrimp is no longer pink. You may want to turn the shrimp once with a spatula while you're cooking to make sure the shrimp are cooked through.

Divide the shrimp among 4 plates or arrange on a platter and serve with linguini or rice.

Serves 4.

Pear Salad ☆☆☆☆☆

1 (10-ounce) bag mixed salad greens or fresh spinach
3 large ripe pears, sliced thinly
1 avocado, sliced thinly
½ cup pine nuts
½ cup Craisins®
1 bottle vinaigrette salad dressing

HERE'S SOME ADVICE ON BUYING and storing pears. They are generally sold rock-hard, but you don't want to eat them that way. Soften them by leaving them out on the counter until they are starting to feel soft near the stems. Then refrigerate them until you're ready to use them.

To make the salad, combine salad greens, pears, avocado slices, pine nuts, and Craisins in a large bowl. Serve with your favorite vinaigrette.

Serves 4 to 6.

Week 16

Using cooked rotisserie chickens can make cooking a whole lot easier. If you don't want to cook and chop chicken yourself, pick up a fat rotisserie chicken at the grocery store that has already been cooked for you. Then you can use a pair of kitchen scissors to quickly cut the cooked chicken into cubes. Don't forget to throw away everything you wouldn't want to find on your plate!

Chicken Curry Salad ☆☆☆☆☆

1   box chicken-flavored Rice-a-Roni®, cooked and cooled
1   whole chicken, cooked and cut into cubes (about 4 cups)
1   (20-ounce) can pineapple chunks, drained
1   (8-ounce) can sliced water chestnuts, drained
1   (8-ounce) package slivered almonds
2   cups red seedless grapes
2   cups celery, chopped
1   tablespoon soy sauce
2   tablespoons lemon juice
1½ cups mayonnaise (don't use salad dressing or Miracle Whip)
2   teaspoons curry powder
½   red onion, thinly sliced

COMBINE THE FIRST SEVEN INGREDIENTS in a large bowl. In a separate bowl, combine soy sauce, lemon juice, mayonnaise and curry powder. Pour the mixture over the salad and chill in the refrigerator.

Stir in the onion just before serving. For optimum taste, chill the salad overnight before serving.

Serves 14.

Hazie's Lazy-Dazy Cake ☆☆☆☆☆

- 2 eggs
- 1 cup sugar
- 1 cup flour
- 1 teaspoon baking powder
- ½ cup milk
  Dollop butter (about the size of a walnut)
- 1 teaspoon vanilla
- 1 recipe Lazy-Dazy Frosting (see below)

GREASE AND FLOUR A 9x13-INCH METAL BAKING PAN. Preheat oven to 325 degrees.

In a large bowl, beat the eggs lightly with a wire whisk. Beat the sugar into the eggs until combined well. In a separate bowl, sift the flour and baking powder together, and then stir it into the egg mixture; set aside. In a small saucepan, heat the milk over low heat until it is just about to boil. Stir constantly to prevent milk from scorching. Add the butter to the hot milk and stir until the butter melts. Immediately pour the hot milk/butter into the flour and egg mixture. Stir in the vanilla. Pour the batter into the prepared pan and bake for 25 to 30 minutes. Prepare Lazy-Dazy Frosting while cake is baking; pour over the cake while the cake is still hot. Return cake to the oven and turn on the broiler to brown the coconut. Watch carefully, so you don't burn the cake.

Serves 12 to 16.

Lazy-Dazy Frosting

¼ cup heavy cream
¾ cup (1½ sticks) butter
½ cup brown sugar, packed
1 cup shredded coconut

COMBINE ALL INGREDIENTS in a heavy saucepan over medium-high heat. Bring mixture to a boil, stirring consistantly; maintain boil for 3½ minutes.

Week 17

You've been eating tuna fish sandwiches all your life, but you may have never made one yourself. Here's a primer for you—and the recipe can be used with other meats, such as ham, chicken, salmon, and turkey. These can be purchased in cans, just like tuna, or you can do something different with leftover meat of any of those varieties. Once the meat mixture is complete, you can put it on bread or serve it many different ways.

Tuna Salad / Tuna Sandwiches ☆☆☆☆☆

THERE ARE ONLY TWO THINGS THAT MUST BE included in every tuna salad: tuna and some sort of glue to hold everything together. For the tuna, you can select water-packed or oil-packed tuna, chunk light, chunk dark, or solid albacore. There are many kinds of glue: mayonnaise, flavored mayonnaise, Miracle Whip, olive oil, mustard, or anything else you want. All that matters is that you mix drained tuna with your chosen glue, adding the glue until the salad reaches the desired consistency. Start with a tablespoon of glue for each drained can of meat, and then add more until you get what you want. Serve the whole concoction over lettuce, on crackers, as a filling for avocados, or between slices of bread. If there's any one meal that allows for unlimited adaptations, tuna salad is it.

Although the only necessary ingredients for tuna salad are tuna and glue, most people add other ingredients, such as: jalapeños, chopped onion, pickle relish, hard-boiled eggs, diced tomatoes, pimientos, olives (green or black), capers, chopped green onion, chopped celery, chopped apple, raisins, cranberries, slivered almonds, pecans, diced carrots, frozen peas (thawed), croutons, chives, salsa, crumbled potato chips, crumbled tortilla chips, garlic, or other spices.

This list is by no means comprehensive. You can experiment to find a favorite combination of ingredients, but even then you'll want some variety. Vary the recipe depending on your mood and the available ingredients.

Corn Chowder ☆☆☆☆☆

   3   slices bacon
   1   small onion, thinly sliced and separated into rings
   1   medium potato, peeled and diced
  ¼   cup water
   1   (14.75-ounce) can cream-style corn
   1   cup milk
  ½   teaspoon salt
       Dash black pepper
       Butter

IN A MEDIUM SAUCEPAN, cook the bacon until crisp. Remove bacon and drain on paper towels; crumble and set aside. Pour off all but 2 tablespoons of the bacon grease. Add the onion slices to the saucepan and cook over medium heat until lightly browned. Add the diced potato and water; cook over medium heat until potato is tender, 10 to 15 minutes. Stir in corn, milk, salt, and pepper. Cook until heated through. Top each serving with crumbled bacon and a pat of butter.

Serves 2 to 4.

Week 18

This first recipe looks like a long one, but you can rid yourself of most of the work if you can find pre-made meatballs in your grocer's freezer. If you can't find pre-made meatballs, don't worry. Making meatballs is easy. This recipe is a snap, and the results are good enough that you can serve them to guests.

You'll also notice that two of the recipes call for ginger root. This is fresh ginger, not the kind sold in a jar in the spice aisle. Ginger root is found in the produce section of your supermarket. When you are ready to use it you'll need to peel it with a vegetable peeler and chop it very finely.

As for the salad, if you don't want to make the dressing—don't. Buy a good, bottled dressing and go from there.

Japanese Meatballs ☆☆☆☆☆

2   pounds lean ground meat (beef, chicken, or turkey)
1   tablespoon finely chopped ginger root
½   cup cornstarch
¼   cup water
¾   teaspoon salt
2   tablespoons vegetable oil
1   recipe Meatball Sauce (see below)

IF YOU ARE USING PRE-MADE MEATBALLS, simply thaw and heat according to package directions; set aside.

If you're making your own meatballs, combine meat, ginger, cornstarch, water, and salt in a large bowl and mix well with your hands. (You'll obviously want to wash your hands and remove your jewelry before you play with your food!) To make the meatballs, simply tear off pieces of the meat mixture and form 1-inch balls.

Heat the oil in a large skillet over medium-high heat. Test the oil by placing a meatball in it. If it sizzles and pops, the oil is hot enough to begin frying the meatballs. Place the meatballs in the hot oil, leaving a little room between balls. When meatballs are nicely browned on one side, turn them over to brown the other sides. You will probably need to fry the meatballs in batches. When the first batch is cooked, remove with a slotted spoon and drain on paper towels. Fry remaining meatballs; set aside while you make the Meatball Sauce.

Return your meatballs to the skillet. Pour the Meatball Sauce over the meatballs and cook over medium heat, stirring constantly until the sauce thickens to gravy consistency. Serve hot over rice, or as an appetizer without rice. If you serve them as an appetizer, make sure to have a lot of toothpicks on hand!

Serves 4 to 12.

Meatball Sauce

1 tablespoon finely chopped ginger root
2 tablespoons chopped green onions (green tops only)
⅔ cup sugar
½ cup soy sauce
½ cup vinegar
3 tablespoons rice vinegar
¼ cup water
2 tablespoons cornstarch

COMBINE ALL INGREDIENTS in a large bowl and mix well, stirring until mixture is smooth.

Oriental Salad ☆☆☆☆☆

1 (1-pound) bag precut coleslaw
1 cup slivered almonds
1 bunch green onions, washed and chopped (tops and bottoms)
1 (12-ounce) can chow mein noodles
1 recipe Oriental Dressing (see below)

Toss coleslaw, almonds, green onions, and chow mein noodles together in a large bowl. Shake Oriental Dressing or bottled salad dressing, then pour over salad and toss again. Serve immediately.

Serves 4 to 8.

Oriental Dressing

¼ cup sugar
½ teaspoon black pepper
¾ cup salad or cooking oil
1 teaspoon salt
3 tablespoons rice vinegar
1 teaspoon sesame oil
½ teaspoon chili oil (optional)

Place all ingredients in a canning jar or other container with a lid and shake well, until oil and vinegar are emulsified (which simply means that they are completely incorporated). Store unused dressing in the refrigerator for up to 4 weeks.

Week 19

The first part of May brings Cinco de Mayo (May 5th), which is a big celebration in Mexico. Celebrate with your own Mexican fiesta.

Taco Casserole ☆☆☆☆☆

1   (15-ounce) bag Fritos®, crushed
2   (15-ounce) cans chili
1   large sweet onion, chopped
3   cups shredded cheddar cheese

PREHEAT OVEN TO 350 DEGREES. Avoid a mess by crushing the Fritos in their own unopened bag. Put a layer (about a half-inch thick) of crushed chips on the bottom of a casserole dish. Cover the chips with a thin layer of chili, then a thin layer of onion over the chili, and then a thin layer of cheese on the top. Keep layering in that order until you get to the top of the casserole dish. Bake for 30 minutes, until heated through and bubbly.

Serves 4 to 6.

Nachos ☆☆☆☆☆

Tortilla chips
Shredded cheddar cheese
Other ingredients of your choice:
Browned ground meat or shredded cooked chicken
Sliced or chopped jalapeño peppers (these come in jars and
    can be found in the Mexican food section of your market)

Chopped tomatoes

Salsa

Sliced black olives

Chopped green onion (white part and the green tops)

ARRANGE TORTILLA CHIPS on a cookie sheet. Top chips with cheese and other ingredients of your choice. Cook under the broiler until the cheese melts. Serve alone or with guacamole or sour cream.

Quesadillas ☆☆☆☆☆

QUESADILLAS ARE LIKE NACHOS, except you use flour tortillas instead of tortilla chips—sort of like a Mexican pizza. Refer to the recipe for nachos for possible quesadilla toppings, but remember that tortillas are too thin for too many heavy items. (If you want to make a taco pizza, use a regular pizza crust.)

Quesadillas may be made by putting your ingredients on top of one tortilla (open face), or by putting a tortilla on the top and the bottom, like a sandwich. If you do not have a tortilla on top, put the quesadilla on a cookie sheet under the broiler until the cheese melts. If you do have a tortilla on top, bake the whole thing in a 350-degree oven until the cheese melts. Another option is to put a small amount of butter in a frying pan and cook the quesadilla on one side and then the other—until the cheese is melted and the tortillas are golden brown.

Serves 4 to 6.

Week 20

Now that you know how to make tuna salad sandwiches, you can stretch your wings and try a tuna melt sandwich. This recipe works for ham salad, chicken salad, or turkey salad too. Experiment! And be sure to try this Waldorf salad recipe. It's the best one we've ever tasted.

Tuna Melt Sandwiches ☆☆☆☆☆

      Tuna salad (see page 38)
  2   slices bread
2 to 3   slices cheese

THIS OPEN-FACE SANDWICH combines the best features of tuna salad and grilled cheese sandwiches. Put tuna salad on bread slices, top with a slice or 2 of cheese, and put the sandwich under the broiler until the cheese melts. You may want to put the sandwiches closer to the middle of the oven than you would usually do with broiled food, and you may want to close the oven door, even though the oven setting is still on broil. This is so the tuna salad will get warm before the cheese burns. Be sure to put the sandwich on a cookie sheet before you put it in the oven, otherwise you'll have tuna salad all over the bottom of your oven. By the way, don't just make tuna melts on white bread with American cheese. Experiment with different cheese varieties, and use exotic breads for the base. A piece of pita bread makes a great tuna melt pizza, and you can't beat a tuna melt using a baguette that's been sliced in half.

Serves 2.

Waldorf Salad ☆☆☆☆☆

    5   cups diced apples
    3   cups diced celery
 2½   cups broken pecans (not walnuts!)
 1¼   cups raisins
    ½   cup mayonnaise (not salad dressing!)
    2   tablespoons sugar
    1   teaspoon lemon juice
        Dash salt
        1 pint unsweetened heavy cream, whipped

COMBINE APPLES, CELERY, PECANS, and raisins in a large bowl. In a separate, small bowl, blend mayonnaise, sugar, lemon juice, and salt. Fold the mayonnaise mixture into the apple mixture. Fold in whipped cream. Chill. If you're lucky enough to have leftovers, this salad tastes great for breakfast.

Serves about 13 (recipe yields 9 cups salad).

Week 21

Ginger chicken is a favorite chicken dish. The pineapple rings and maraschino cherries add festiveness. Speaking of pineapple rings and maraschino cherries, wouldn't pineapple upside-down cake be a nice way to end the meal? Consider it done!

Ginger Chicken ☆☆☆☆☆

4   boneless, skinless chicken breasts
¼   cup bottled teriyaki sauce or teriyaki marinade
1   tablespoon soy sauce
2   tablespoons orange juice
4   cloves finely chopped garlic
2   tablespoons finely minced ginger root
4   canned pineapple rings
4   maraschino cherries

ARRANGE CHICKEN BREASTS in a square glass baking pan. Combine teriyaki sauce, soy sauce, orange juice, garlic, and ginger in a small bowl. (For details on fresh ginger, see the note on page 40 on Week 18.) Pour the teriyaki mixture over the chicken and cover with aluminum foil. Refrigerate 1 hour. Turn over chicken breasts, replace the foil, and refrigerate another hour. With the foil still in place, cook at 350 degrees for 25 minutes. Spoon juices over the chicken, replace foil, and bake for 25 minutes more. Put a slice of pineapple on each piece of chicken, and a maraschino cherry in the center of the slice.

Spoon juices over the chicken again and bake, uncovered, another 10 minutes. Serve with steamed rice or fried rice.

Serves 4.

Fried Rice ☆☆☆☆☆

¼	cup vegetable oil
5	cups cooked rice
2	green onions with tops, washed and chopped
	Fresh mushrooms (a handful or so), sliced
2 to 3	eggs
2	tablespoons soy sauce
1	cup frozen peas, thawed

HEAT THE OIL IN A LARGE SKILLET or pot over medium heat. Add the rice and sauté in oil for 5 minutes, stirring occasionally. Stir in green onions and mushrooms. Continue cooking for several minutes to cook the mushrooms. Add eggs and soy sauce to the pan, and stir until eggs are broken up and cooked. Stir in peas and serve.

Serves 6.

Pineapple Upside-Down Cake ☆☆☆☆☆

⅔ cup butter
¾ cup brown sugar, packed
1 (16-ounce) can pineapple rings
   Maraschino cherries (one cherry per pineapple ring)
   Pecan halves (optional)
1 box yellow cake mix, prepared according to package
   directions

PREHEAT OVEN TO 375 DEGREES. Place the butter and brown sugar in a glass, rectangular baking dish and place the dish in the oven until the butter melts and the sugar dissolves. Remove the dish and place pineapple rings in the butter and sugar mixture. Put a cherry in the center of each pineapple ring, and perhaps one between the rings. (You could also put pecan halves in the spaces between the pineapple rings.) Pour the cake batter over the pineapple and cherries. Bake for about 35 minutes. Let cool for 5 minutes, then loosen the edges with a knife and turn the cake over onto a large tray or cookie sheet. Serve with whipped cream, or just eat it fresh from the oven.

Serves 10 to 12.

Week 22

This first recipe makes healthy and delicious potatoes or shrimp, and the second recipe will turn an ordinary bag of frozen corn into an amazing side dish.

Crabby Potatoes (or Boiled Shrimp) ☆☆☆☆☆

3 to 4   pounds small red potatoes (golf ball size)
   1   box crab boil (see Appendix B for more info on this ingredient)
  ¼   cup salt
   1   lemon, cut in half (for shrimp only)
   4   pounds shrimp (optional)

ALTHOUGH PEOPLE ARE ALWAYS SAYING that potatoes are healthier without toppings, they just aren't as good without a big dollop of butter or cheese. But here's a recipe that produces great-tasting potatoes without butter.

Fill a large pot two-thirds full of water, and throw in about a quarter-cup of salt. You don't have to measure; just throw it in. Add the bag of crab boil right out of the box. Now put the pot on a burner and turn the heat to medium-high.

Wash the potatoes in cold water, cleaning the skins thoroughly with a vegetable scrubber. Put the potatoes all at once in the soup pot. You may want to add a tablespoon of oil so the water doesn't boil over.

Boil the potatoes until a fork inserted in the largest one doesn't meet any resistance. The crab boil should smell strong and spicy. When the potatoes are done, drain out the water, put the potatoes in a bowl, and refrigerate them until they're cold. You may want to cook them the day before you eat them. Serve them as is or with a little seasoning salt. They should keep for many days if covered and kept in the refrigerator. This is a terrific dish during the hot days of summer because the potatoes are served cold.

Once you know how to cook crabby potatoes, you can boil shrimp. In fact, some people cook the potatoes in the shrimp water after cooking the shrimp, because the potatoes pick up the flavor. If you're cooking shrimp, add a lemon—cut in half—to the water. This will keep the shells from sticking to the shrimp. Cook the shrimp in their shells according to the directions on the crab boil box.

Serves 6 to 8.

Daryl's Fried Corn ☆☆☆☆☆

¼ cup (½ stick) butter
1 large onion, chopped
1 (16-ounce) bag frozen corn
   Salt, to taste
   Black pepper, to taste

MELT THE BUTTER OVER MEDIUM HEAT in a large skillet. Sauté the onion in the butter until the onions are translucent and soft; add the frozen corn. Cook, stirring occasionally, until the water from the corn has evaporated so that you're left with onions and corn and butter. Add salt and pepper to taste, and serve.

Serves 4 to 6.

Week 23

Just about the most expensive salad you can get in a restaurant is Shrimp Louie. These salads are much cheaper to make at home, and they're insanely easy to do. Follow up the Shrimp Louie with a hot baked apple, and your meal will be complete.

Shrimp Louie ☆☆☆☆☆

1 cup cooked shrimp per person
   Seafood Magic® spice blend (optional)
2 cups salad greens per person
   Tomato wedges (optional)
2 boiled eggs per person, sliced or cut into wedges
¼ cup black olives per person
   Lemon wedges (optional)
   Thousand Island Dressing (see below)

IF YOU WANT TO USE FRESH SHRIMP in this recipe, you can follow the directions in the Crabby Potatoes recipe to cook the shrimp. Otherwise, buy frozen, cooked shrimp from your grocery store. Thaw the shrimp. If you have Seafood Magic on hand, lightly sprinkle some on the shrimp. Arrange the ingredients on the plate in this order: salad greens, tomatoes, eggs, olives, lemon wedges, shrimp. Add Thousand Island salad dressing and serve.

If you really want to splurge you can substitute an equal amount of crab meat for the shrimp and omit the Seafood Magic.

Thousand Island Dressing, Fry Sauce, or "Special Sauce" ☆☆☆☆☆

   1   cup mayonnaise (not Miracle Whip)
   ¼   cup ketchup
1 to 2   tablespoons sweet pickle relish (for Thousand Island
            dressing only)

THIS IS AN EASY RECIPE for making your own Thousand Island Dressing, and it is much cheaper than the prepared dressings. Use it on a seafood Louie, with French fries, or with any salad. In a small bowl, mix mayonnaise with ketchup until the mixture is a pale coral color. If you're making fry sauce, you're finished! If you're making Thousand Island Dressing, add a tablespoon or two of drained pickle relish. Store leftover dressing in a jar or some other covered container, and keep it in the refrigerator. This is ideal for your iceberg lettuce salads, or to make your own version of that "special sauce" used on many fast-food hamburgers.

Melanie's Baked Apples ☆☆☆☆☆

1 package Pillsbury® crescent rolls
2 apples, peeled, quartered, and cored
¼ cup (½ stick) butter, melted
¾ cup sugar
½ teaspoon cinnamon
½ teaspoon nutmeg
1 (12-ounce) can lemon-lime soda

PREHEAT OVEN TO 350 DEGREES. Roll out one crescent roll for each apple piece. (You can roll out the crescent roll with a drinking glass if you don't have a rolling pin.) Then wrap the dough around the apple quarters. Pinch the seams closed as much as possible. (It's fine if there are exposed pieces of apple.) Place each apple bundle seam-side down in a baking dish. Pour melted butter over the apple bundles. In a small bowl, combine sugar, cinnamon, and nutmeg, then sprinkle the mixture over the buttered apples. Pour half of the lemon-lime soda over the mixture. (You can drink or discard the rest.) Bake until browned and bubbly, about 10 to 12 minutes. Serve hot with vanilla ice cream or whipped cream.

Serves 8.

Week 24

There are many enchilada recipes, and many ways to cook rice. But these are absolutely the best recipes we've found for either enchiladas or rice, and they're both easy to make. The only possible way you can mess these recipes up is to substitute ingredients in the enchiladas. DO NOT EVEN THINK ABOUT MAKING ANY SUBSTITUTIONS! And that includes virtuously substituting low-fat ingredients for the high-fat ones. If you want something healthy, make a salad. These recipes are for use when you want a sinfully rich meal to impress friends!

Kim's Chicken Enchiladas ☆☆☆☆☆

1 tablespoon butter
1 large onion, chopped
1 (4.5-ounce) can chopped green chilies, drained
1 (8-ounce) package cream cheese, softened
3½ cups chopped, cooked chicken breast
8 (8-inch) flour tortillas
2 (8-ounce) blocks Monterey Jack cheese, shredded
2 cups heavy cream

PREHEAT OVEN TO 350 DEGREES. Melt the butter in a large skillet over medium heat. Add the chopped onion and sauté in the butter for five minutes. Add the green chilies and sauté for one minute. Cube the softened cream cheese and stir it in to the onion mixture, along with the chicken; cook, stirring constantly, until the cream cheese melts.

Spoon 2 to 3 tablespoons of the chicken mixture down the center of each tortilla. Roll up each tortilla and place it, seam-side down, in a lightly greased 9x13-inch baking dish. When all the tortillas are in the baking dish, sprinkle Monterey Jack cheese on the top and then drizzle with the cream. Bake for 45 minutes.

Serves 4 to 8 (makes 8 enchiladas).

Salvadoran Rice ☆☆☆☆☆

   Vegetable oil
1 large onion, chopped
1 bell pepper, deseeded and chopped
8 large mushrooms, sliced
1 (5-ounce) bottle green olives stuffed with pimientos
2 teaspoons salt
1 quart chicken broth
1 tablespoon capers
2 cups long grain rice

POUR ¼ INCH VEGETABLE OIL in a large skillet and heat over medium heat. Add the onions and sauté for 5 minutes or so. Add the bell pepper and the mushrooms. Cook and stir until the onions are translucent and the peppers are limp. Drain off the oil. Drain the juice from the olives and slice each olive into 3 to 5 pieces. Add salt, olives, chicken broth, and capers to the vegetables in the skillet. Bring the mixture to a boil and cook for 2 minutes. Add the rice, but don't stir. Boil the mixture, uncovered, until the liquid cooks down and the rice is no longer covered by liquid. Reduce heat to low, cover the pan, and cook for an additional 20 minutes.

Serves 6 to 8.

Week 25

There is no more basic dinner than a meatloaf dinner. This is comfort food that will make you feel good when you've had a miserable day— or even when you haven't. Serve with Green Bean and Onion Casserole. With food like this, you'll look for excuses to be comforted.

Botchie's Meatloaf ☆☆☆☆☆

2	slices bread
½	cup milk
1	teaspoon chili powder
1½	teaspoons salt
½	teaspoon black pepper
1	medium onion, diced
1	(15-ounce) can diced tomatoes
1	pound very lean ground meat (beef, chicken, turkey)
	Red or white potatoes, peeled and halved

PREHEAT OVEN TO 400 DEGREES. Tear the bread into bite-sized pieces and place them in a large mixing bowl. Add milk, chili powder, salt, pepper, and diced onion. Open the can of diced tomatoes and drain it into a container so you can use the liquid later in the recipe. Add the drained tomatoes to the milk mixture. Add the ground meat and work the whole mixture together with your hands. Form it into a mound and place it in a large casserole dish. Put potato halves around the outside of the mound. Pour the liquid from the drained tomatoes around and over the potatoes and meat. Bake, covered, for about 30 minutes; remove the cover and cook another

30 minutes. The meatloaf is done when the meat is no longer pink in the center of the mound, and the potatoes are tender but not mushy.

Serves 4.

Green Bean and Onion Casserole ☆☆☆☆☆

1 (10.75-ounce) can cream of mushroom soup
½ cup milk
1 teaspoon soy sauce
Dash black pepper
4 cups cooked green beans (French-style is preferred)
1½ cups (2.8-ounce can) French's® French-Fried Onions

PREHEAT OVEN TO 350 DEGREES. Mix soup, milk, soy sauce, pepper, beans, and half of the fried onions in a casserole dish. Bake 25 minutes, or until heated through. Stir mixture and then sprinkle remaining onions on the top. Bake for another 5 minutes, or until onions are golden brown.

Serves 4.

Week 26

Monte Cristo sandwiches are usually served in upscale restaurants, but there's no law that says you can't make them at home. Add some easy pasta salad, and you have the perfect ingredients for a party.

Easy Pasta Salad ☆☆☆☆☆

1	(16-ounce) package shell pasta (or other pasta varieties), cooked, drained, and chilled
⅓	cup mayonnaise
1	can sliced black olives, drained
4 to 6	sliced green onions and tops or 1 sweet onion, chopped
1	carrot, chopped
1	pound salad shrimp, thawed, or diced ham (optional)

STIR CHILLED PASTA WITH A FORK so there aren't any clumps of pasta sticking together. Stir in mayonnaise. If the mixture seems to need more "glue," add more mayonnaise, a tablespoon at a time. Add other ingredients. Stir. Add salt and pepper to taste, and stir again. Chill and serve. If you add the shrimp or maybe even diced ham, this will be festive enough for a party.

See Appendix A if you need help cooking the pasta.

Serves 6 to 8.

Monte Cristo Sandwiches ☆☆☆☆☆

1	large loaf French bread
1	egg per sandwich

Salt, to taste

Black pepper, to taste

2   teaspoons water or milk

1   tablespoon Dijon mustard per sandwich

1   tablespoon butter, softened, per sandwich, plus more for
    cooking the sandwiches

White cheese (Swiss, provolone, or mozzarella)

Thinly sliced turkey

Thinly sliced ham

CUT THE BREAD INTO SLICES three-fourths to one-inch thick, and set aside. Into a large bowl, break the eggs. Shake in a little salt and pepper and add two teaspoons of water or milk. Beat the mixture with a fork to break the yolk and combine ingredients.

Use approximately one tablespoon each of mustard and soft butter per sandwich. Take two slices of bread and spread the butter on one side of one slice, and the mustard on one side of the other slice. On top of the buttered side of the bread put a couple slices of turkey, a slice of cheese, and a couple slices of ham. Top with the mustard side of the other piece of bread; your sandwich is constructed.

Preheat oven to 350 degrees. Melt a small amount of butter in a frying pan over medium heat. Quickly dip the sandwich in the bowl of egg mixture so that the bread is completely covered. Place in the pan and brown—not burn—the sandwich on both sides. Repeat for each sandwich you wish to make. When all the sandwiches are made, put them on a cookie sheet in the oven for 3 to 4 minutes to melt the cheese. Slice each sandwich in half and serve.

Week 27

A summertime picnic can be successful even if you don't have a barbecue grill. Here's a recipe for baby back ribs, along with instructions on how to make a delicious potato salad. And if you still have room for dessert, we have a recipe for that too.

Baby Back Ribs ☆☆☆☆☆

4	pounds baby back pork ribs
1	whole head of garlic, chopped or put through a garlic press
3	tablespoons oregano
1	teaspoon cayenne pepper
2	teaspoons seasoning salt
¼	cup vegetable oil
1	bottle barbecue sauce (optional)

PREHEAT THE OVEN TO 400 DEGREES. Place the ribs side by side in a glass baking dish or a roasting pan. Combine garlic, oregano, cayenne, seasoning salt, and oil in a medium bowl and mix well. Cover both sides of the ribs with the garlic and oregano mixture, coating each rib evenly.

Roast in the oven for one hour, flipping each rib once after 30 minutes. If you want to add barbecue sauce, brush it on both sides of the ribs about five minutes before the end of cooking. Remove the dish, cover it with foil, and let it rest for 10 minutes.

Serves 4.

Crunchy Potato Salad ☆☆☆☆☆

12 red or white potatoes

3 eggs

1 large sweet onion, chopped

1 cup chopped carrots

1 cup chopped celery

2 tablespoons mustard

1½ cups mayonnaise (not Miracle Whip!)

½ cup milk

1 teaspoon celery salt

1 teaspoon parsley flakes

PLACE THE WHOLE EGGS AND POTATOES (peeled, if you want, or with the peels on for more color) in the bottom of a large pot. Cover with water and set over high heat. Bring to a boil; reduce heat slightly to maintain a boil but prevent water from boiling over. Boil eggs and potatoes for about 20 minutes, or until you can stick a fork through the largest potato without any resistance. Remove from heat. After the potatoes have cooled, chop them into bite-sized chunks and put in a large bowl. Peel and chop or slice the eggs and add them to the mixture. Add in the chopped onions, carrots, and celery.

Combine the remaining ingredients in a small bowl and mix thoroughly to get rid of lumps. Add this to the potato mixture and blend so that all the ingredients are mixed thoroughly. Add seasoning salt to taste. Chill before serving and keep leftovers refrigerated.

Serves 14.

Fruit and Fluff ☆☆☆☆☆

1   (10-ounce) jar marshmallow fluff
1   (8-ounce) tub fruit-flavored cream cheese, at room
        temperature
    Fresh fruit of your choice, cut into bite-sized pieces

WITH AN ELECTRIC MIXER or wire whisk, mix marshmallow fluff and cream cheese in a small bowl until all the lumps are gone. Serve this as a dip with your choice of fresh fruit. Fruits that work particularly well include apple slices, banana slices, cantaloupe slices, pineapple chunks, and strawberries. Slice bananas and apples at the last minute to minimize browning.

Week 28

Even though they contain cooked chicken and gravy, Hawaiian Haystacks seem cooler than regular hot meals. They are easy to make and and great for guests as everyone gets a customized dinner by adding their favorite ingredients. Finish off the menu with a batch of Cake Mix Cookies, and you've got a dinner that is a summertime favorite.

Hawaiian Haystacks ☆☆☆☆☆

1   cup cooked rice per serving
½   cup cooked, cubed chicken per serving
½   cup Easy Chicken Gravy per serving (see below)
    Toppings (you choose):
    Pineapple tidbits, drained
    Raisins
    Shredded coconut
    Chinese chow mein noodles
    Shredded cheddar cheese
    Green onions, diced
    Frozen peas, thawed but not cooked
    Cashews or slivered almonds
    Diced tomatoes
    Sliced raw mushrooms
    Green pepper, chopped
    Sliced water chestnuts

TO MAKE THIS MEAL AS SIMPLE AS POSSIBLE, buy a cooked rotisserie chicken, remove the meat you'd like to use, and chop it up. To serve, place all the toppings listed above in bowls on the table. Have guests put rice on their plates, topped with chicken and then gravy. Then they can sprinkle on whichever toppings appeal to them.

Easy Chicken Gravy

2 (10.75-ounce) cans cream of chicken soup
1 (14-ounce) can chicken broth
¼ teaspoon garlic powder

COMBINE INGREDIENTS IN A SMALL SAUCEPAN and warm together, adding more chicken broth to reach the consistency you want.

Serves 8.

Cake Mix Cookies ☆☆☆☆☆

1 box cake mix
2 eggs, beaten with a fork
½ cup vegetable oil
1 to 2 cups chocolate chips, nuts, raisins, or whatever else you like in your cookies

IF THIS IS YOUR FIRST ATTEMPT at Cake Mix Cookies, try using devil's food cake mix and white chocolate chips. As you experiment, you'll find that some flavors make better cookies than others. Preheat oven to 350 degrees. Mix eggs and vegetable oil in a large bowl. Stir in cake mix. Add whatever you're mixing in (chocolate chips, nuts, etc.). Drop dough by teaspoonfuls onto an ungreased cookie sheet, about 2 inches apart. Bake 8 to 10 minutes, making sure they don't burn.

Makes 2 to 3 dozen cookies.

Week 29

Summer is a good time for Mexican food, so we'll show you how to make tacos and some refreshing guacamole as a side dish.

Tacos

1   pound ground meat (beef, chicken, or turkey)
1   package taco seasoning (optional)
1   package flour tortillas or crunchy corn taco shells
1   jar salsa or picanté sauce
    Any of the following for toppings:
    Chopped tomatoes
    Shredded lettuce
    Grated cheese
    Chopped onions (white or green)
    Chopped olives
    Sliced jalapeño peppers
    Sour cream

THE ONLY INGREDIENT THAT *has* to be included in a taco is a tortilla or taco shell. You can have a peanut butter and jelly taco if you want.

But to make a traditional taco, you start by browning a pound of ground meat. For a more authentic flavor, cook that meat with a package of taco seasoning. This is available in the Mexican food section of your supermarket (or in the packaged seasoning mix section), and there should be easy directions on the package.

Assemble the optional ingredients in separate bowls, so people can pick and choose what they want to eat. Remove the meat from the heat and drain in a colander.

If you're using prepared corn taco shells, you don't need to heat them before serving.

You can warm the flour tortillas in a microwave, leaving them in the open plastic bag, for about a minute. Or you can wrap several of them in paper towels and cook them for a minute. If you don't have a microwave, heat the tortillas in your oven, with a damp paper towel over the baking dish to keep them from drying out. You can also warm them one at a time in an ungreased frying pan that's large enough to accommodate them.

Now you're ready to fill the tortillas or taco shells with any of the ingredients that look appealing. If you have leftovers, seal them separately in little plastic storage bags. You can heat up the meat, drain the juice off the tomatoes, and mix everything together tomorrow for a taco salad.

Serves 4.

Guacamole ☆☆☆☆☆

3	avocados
1 to 2	tablespoons minced sweet onion
¼	teaspoon salt
1 to 2	tablespoons fresh lemon or lime juice
½	teaspoon ground cumin (optional)
¼	teaspoon cayenne pepper (optional)
2 to 4	tablespoons chopped cilantro (optional)
¼	cup chopped tomatoes (optional)

CUT THE AVOCADOS IN HALF, remove the pit and any bad (brown) spots, and scoop out the green avocado meat with a spoon. Chop the avocado and add to a small bowl. Stir in minced onion, salt, and lime or lemon juice (the juice keeps the avocado from turning brown). Stir in any of the optional ingredients, according to your taste. If you'd prefer a smoother guacamole, smash some of the avocado with a fork before stirring in the optional ingredients. Serve with tortilla chips.

A note about cilantro: Cilantro is a kind of Mexican parsley found in the produce section of your supermarket. It has a lot of flavor, so some might want to use it sparingly! Some people love cilantro, but others hate it. It's a genetic thing; if it tastes like soap to you today, it will always taste like soap to you.

See Appendix A for hints on buying and storing avocados.

Makes about 2½ cups.

Week 30

If you don't have enough time to think about cooking, then let the oven and the refrigerator do the work for you. This terrific chicken recipe takes care of itself in the oven, while the cookies are chilling in the refrigerator. You can even make the salad a day ahead of time and let it sit in the refrigerator until you're ready to eat. It doesn't get any easier than this.

Chicken Parmesan

1 (26-ounce) jar spaghetti sauce
½ cup of grated Parmesan cheese
6 boneless, skinless chicken breasts
2 cups shredded mozzarella cheese
1 pound spaghetti or linguini noodles, cooked

PREHEAT OVEN TO 375 DEGREES. Pour the spaghetti sauce into a 9x13-inch glass baking dish. Stir in half of the Parmesan cheese. Add the chicken breasts, turning them over several times to coat them with the sauce. Cover the dish with aluminum foil and bake for 30 minutes. Remove from the oven, remove the foil, and stir in noodles. Sprinkle with the remaining Parmesan and mozzarella cheeses. Return the dish to the oven without the aluminum foil, and bake for 30 more minutes.

See Appendix A if you have questions about cooking noodles or other pasta.

Serves 6.

Cucumber Salad ☆☆☆☆☆

2 large, ripe tomatoes
1 large cucumber
1 large green pepper
1 small red onion, sliced thinly
¼ cup bottled Greek salad dressing
 Juice of one-half lemon
1 teaspoon dried oregano
½ cup crumbled feta cheese

WASH THE TOMATOES and cut them into wedges. Scrub the cucumber and cut it into thin slices, no more than a quarter of an inch thick. Scrub the green pepper and cut it into bite-sized pieces.

Put all the ingredients in a large bowl and toss them together. Refrigerate up to 24 hours before serving. Serve chilled.

Serves 4 to 6.

Bird's Nest Cookies ☆☆☆☆☆

1 (12-ounce) bag butterscotch chips or chocolate chips
1 (12-ounce) can Chinese noodles
1 cup miniature marshmallows

MELT THE BUTTERSCOTCH OR CHOCOLATE CHIPS in the microwave in a medium bowl. To do so, microwave on high power for 1 minute and stir. Return to microwave in 30-second increments, stirring each time, until melted and smooth. If you don't have a microwave, bring a saucepan of water to a simmer over the stovetop. Place the butterscotch or chocolate chips in a bowl that is large enough to make contact around the edge of the pan and put the bowl on top of the saucepan. Stir until melted. The simmering water will heat the bowl and melt the chips; just make sure the water never reaches a full boil or splashes into the bowl.

When all the chips are melted and the mixture is smooth, add the remaining ingredients and stir well. Use a tablespoon to drop the batter onto a cookie sheet that has been lined with waxed paper. Refrigerate until the cookies are firm.

Makes 2 dozen cookies.

Week 31

Summer just isn't a great time to cook, but for some reason we persist in being hungry anyway. One way to beat the summer heat is with Aluminum Foil Dinners, which can be cooked in the oven, on a barbecue grill, or even in the coals of a campfire. Hazie's Baked Beans are as easy as baked beans can get, but they taste like you slaved over a hot stove for hours.

Aluminum Foil Dinners ☆☆☆☆☆

       Heavy-duty aluminum foil
4   small steaks or 4 boneless, skinless chicken breasts
2   carrots, sliced
2   potatoes, sliced
1   onion, sliced and separated into rings
    Salt
    Black pepper
    Garlic powder
4   slices white cheese (Swiss or Monterey Jack)

TEAR OFF 4 PIECES OF ALUMINUM FOIL, about 18x18 inches. In the center of each piece, place a piece of meat. Stack sliced carrots, potatoes, and onions on top of the meat. Add salt, pepper, and garlic powder to taste. Top with a slice of white cheese. Seal tightly in foil. Bake about 40 minutes on a barbecue grill or in a campfire, or 50 minutes in a 450-degree oven.

Serves 4.

Hazie's Baked Beans ☆☆☆☆☆

1   tablespoon butter
1   cup diced onion
2   1-pound cans baked beans (Bush's® baked beans are good)
6   tablespoons dark molasses
¾   cup ketchup

PREHEAT OVEN TO 350 DEGREES. Melt butter in a large skillet over medium heat. Add onions and sauté until translucent. Transfer onions to a casserole dish. Pour most of the liquid off the cans of beans and add them to the onions. Stir in molasses and ketchup. Bake for at least 25 minutes, until beans are bubbly and piping hot.

Serves 4.

Caramel Krisps ☆☆☆☆☆

3   tablespoons butter
4   cups miniature marshmallows
½   cup caramel ice cream topping
6   cups Kellogg's® Rice Krispies® cereal

MELT THE BUTTER IN LARGE SAUCEPAN over low heat. Add the marshmallows and stir until completely melted. Remove from heat. Add caramel topping, stirring until well mixed. Add the cereal and stir until it is well coated. Butter a 9x13-inch baking dish. Pour in the cereal mixture and press it into pan with a buttered spatula. Cool, and then cut into 24 squares.

Makes 24 bars.

Week 32

If you liked the Aluminum Foil Dinners you made last week, try them Oriental-style this week. Make some Condensed Milk Fudge and you've got yourself food for a party. Invite some friends over to play board games and have yourself a great evening.

Oriental Foil Dinners ☆☆☆☆☆

	Heavy-duty aluminum foil
4	boneless, skinless chicken breasts
¼	cup brown sugar, packed
2	tablespoons soy sauce
½	teaspoon garlic powder
	Dash cayenne pepper
1	(16-ounce) package frozen stir-fry vegetables, thawed
2 to 3	green onions with tops, chopped
4	cups cooked rice

TEAR OFF 4 PIECES OF FOIL, about 18x18 inches each. Cut the chicken breasts into long strips and set them aside. Mix sugar and seasonings in a medium bowl. Add meat, stir-fry vegetables, and chopped green onions; mix well to coat the ingredients with the spice mixture. Place a quarter of the meat mixture on the center of each piece of aluminum foil. Seal the foil tightly around the edges. Bake about 15 minutes on a covered barbecue grill or campfire, or 18 minutes in a 450-degree oven. Serve over hot rice. See Appendix A for instructions on making rice.

Serves 4.

Condensed Milk Fudge ☆☆☆☆☆

1 (14-ounce) can sweetened condensed milk
1 (12-ounce) package chocolate chips
1 cup chopped nuts

HEAT THE CHOCOLATE CHIPS and condensed milk in a medium saucepan over low heat until the chocolate melts. Stir in the nuts. Pour into a buttered 8x8-inch pan and chill for several hours, until hardened.

For possible variations, experiment with dark or milk chocolate chips—or even butterscotch or peanut butter chips. Another variation is using mint chocolate chips to make mint-flavored fudge. If you don't want to put nuts in your fudge, think of substituting toffee bits, miniature marshmallows, or other treats.

Makes 24 pieces.

Week 33

Sometimes when you're buying unusual ingredients for one dish, it makes sense to use those same ingredients in another dish at the same meal. We've done that this week by using coconut in the salad and then adding a coconut cake as a dessert. Now you have a themed dinner—although we wouldn't recommend adding coconut to the Easy Chicken Stroganoff!

Easy Chicken Stroganoff ☆☆☆☆☆

4	boneless, skinless chicken breasts
1 to 2	tablespoons vegetable oil
1	onion, thinly sliced
	Salt, to taste
	Black pepper, to taste
	Garlic powder, to taste
1	(10.75-ounce) can cream of mushroom soup
¾	cup water
1	(8-ounce) carton sour cream
1	(10-ounce) box frozen peas, thawed (optional)
1	(16-ounce) package medium egg noodles, cooked and hot

CUT THE CHICKEN BREASTS into bite-sized pieces; set aside. Heat the oil in a large frying pan over medium-high heat. Add chicken, onion, salt, pepper, and garlic powder to the pan and sauté until chicken is browned and onions are translucent. Add the cream of mushroom soup and a small amount of water to the frying pan. Cook and stir over medium-low heat until heated through. Add the carton of sour cream and the peas, if you are using them. Continue cooking until the dish is heated through. Serve over cooked egg noodles. See Appendix A if you are unsure about how to prepare egg noodles and other types of pasta.

Serves 4.

Five-Cup Ambrosia ☆☆☆☆☆

1 cup shredded, sweetened coconut
1 cup miniature marshmallows
1 (11-ounce) can mandarin orange segments, drained
1 (20-ounce) can sweetened pineapple chunks, drained
1 cup sour cream
  Maraschino cherries or chopped pecans (optional)

COMBINE ALL INGREDIENTS in a large bowl and chill for several hours to mix the flavors before serving.

Serves 4.

Coconut Cake ☆☆☆☆☆

1 box deluxe white cake mix
6 ounces shredded coconut (about 2¼ cups)
1 cup milk
1 cup sugar
½ cup Maraschino cherries, halved (optional)
Whipped cream

PREPARE THE CAKE MIX as directed on the box. Bake the cake in a 9x13-inch baking dish. While the cake is baking, combine the coconut, milk, sugar, and maraschino cherries, if using, in a small bowl; set aside in the refrigerator while the cake bakes. Remove the cake from the oven and pour the coconut mixture evenly over the hot cake. Cover with foil and refrigerate at least three hours (you can make this the day before and keep it refrigerated if you want). Add a dollop of whipped cream to each piece immediately before serving. Store any leftover cake in the refrigerator.

Serves 12 to 16.

Week 34

Everyone likes a good old-fashioned bacon, lettuce, and tomato sandwich. Here's a wrap version, accompanied by tasty Speedy Tomato Pasta.

BLT Wrap Sandwiches ☆☆☆☆☆

2	ripe tomatoes
1	avocado
	Mayonnaise
4	(10-inch) flour tortillas
2	cups mixed salad greens
⅓	cup ranch salad dressing
12	slices bacon, fried crisp (or bacon bits)

WASH AND DICE THE TOMATOES. Cut the avocado in half, remove the pit, and then scoop out the avocado meat from each side with a spoon and slice it thinly. (See Appendix A for tips on buying and storing avocados.) Spread a thin coating of mayonnaise on each tortilla, about 1 or 2 teaspoons per tortilla. Combine the avocado, tomatoes, salad greens, and ranch dressing and mix well. Spread the vegetable mixture on each tortilla so that it runs lengthwise across the tortilla. Top with three pieces of bacon (or some bacon bits). Roll up each tortilla lengthwise into a "tube," just like a fruit roll-up or an enchilada, and place on a serving plate. Serve immediately.

Serves 4.

Speedy Tomato Pasta ☆☆☆☆☆

  1 (16-ounce) bag pasta, cooked according to package
      directions
  1 tablespoon butter or oil
3 or 4 green onions (tops and bottoms), chopped
  1 (8-ounce) package sliced fresh mushrooms
  2 cloves garlic, minced
  1 (14.5-ounce) can Italian tomatoes
  ½ cup grated Parmesan cheese (fresh, or from the can)

SEE APPENDIX A if you need help cooking the pasta. For this recipe, you can use any kind of pasta: bow ties, shells, tubular, and so on. Heat the oil or butter in a large frying pan over medium heat. Sauté the onions, mushrooms, and garlic in the fat until the onions are clear and the garlic is barely tender. Add the tomatoes, and continue cooking until heated thoroughly. Stir in the cooked pasta and sprinkle with cheese before serving.

Serves 4.

Week 35

Sometimes you can use unusual ingredients in recipes and have surprisingly good results. If you're an adventurous person, you can sometimes make these little adjustments to recipes and come up with wonderful variations. Other times, you will wish you had stuck to the original recipe! Our first recipe for this week is a chicken dish that includes a soft drink as one of the ingredients. The second recipe is a little more traditional, but is a wonderful variation on the standard baked potato. Serving them this way might just spoil you, so that you want your potatoes twice-baked every time.

7-UP Chicken ☆☆☆☆☆

1 package chicken parts (3 to 4 pounds), or the same amount of chicken breasts or chicken legs
1 (16-ounce) bottle barbecue sauce
1 (12-ounce) can 7-UP®
Salt, to taste
Black pepper, to taste

PLACE THE CHICKEN PIECES in a skillet. Pour the barbecue sauce and ten ounces of the 7-UP (that's 1¼ cups) over the chicken. (Now live a little; drink the other two ounces!) Simmer the mixture over low heat for 45 minutes, or until tender, turning the chicken occasionally. Season with salt and pepper to taste before serving.

Serves 4.

Twice-Baked Potatoes ☆☆☆☆☆

4   baking potatoes
¾   cup milk
½   cup butter
    Salt, to taste
    Black pepper, to taste
1   cup shredded cheddar cheese

BAKE THE POTATOES. If you don't know how, please refer to Appendix A. When the potatoes are done, take them from the oven and cut off and discard about the top third of each potato, length-wise. The potatoes will be hot, so handle them with a towel or potholder so that you don't burn yourself!

Scoop out as much of the potato pulp as you can, leaving the skin intact. Place the insides of each potato in a large mixing bowl. When complete, the skin of each potato should be shaped like a little empty bowl. Add milk and butter to the potato mixture in the bowl. Mash it up with a fork or an electric mixer. Add some salt and pepper to taste. Stir in the shredded cheese. Stuff the mashed potato filling back into the empty skins, making sure that each potato has about the same amount of stuffing. Sprinkle the top of each potato with remaining cheddar cheese and return potatoes to the oven just long enough to melt the cheese. Serve immediately.

Serves 4.

Week 36

Packaged or canned ingredients can often be used when creating recipes that taste better than their individual ingredients. Here are three recipes that are easily made because a lot of the work has been done for you. Don't be afraid to add your own touches! For example, you can substitute cauliflower for broccoli in Broccoli Cheese Soup, or you can add thawed frozen peas to the soup or the salad. Be creative!

Broccoli Cheese Soup ☆☆☆☆☆

1   (16-ounce) package fresh or frozen broccoli florets
2   tablespoons butter
¼   cup chopped onion
1   (10.75-ounce) can cream of chicken soup
2   cups shredded cheddar cheese
3   cups milk

STEAM THE BROCCOLI until very tender; set aside. In a large pot, melt the butter over medium-high heat and sauté the onion until translucent. Add the soup and stir the mixture over low heat. When heated through, add the cheese and stir until it has melted. Add milk and whip the mixture with a fork until there are no lumps. Add the broccoli and stir. Simmer until the soup bubbles.

Serves 4.

Citrus Salad ☆☆☆☆☆

1   bag salad greens (your favorite variety)
1   jar pink grapefruit sections, drained (in the refrigerator case
     in the produce section)
¼   cup Craisins® (dried cranberries)
¼   cup slivered almonds (on the baking aisle)
     Bottled Italian or Caesar salad dressing

MIX ALL THE INGREDIENTS except for salad dressing. Just before
serving, drizzle on a little salad dressing.

Serves 4.

Pineapple Pie ☆☆☆☆☆

1   refrigerated or frozen pie shell in a pie tin (buy in the frozen
     foods section of the supermarket)
1   (20-ounce) can crushed pineapple, drained
1   (3.4-ounce) box vanilla instant pudding, made into pudding
     Juice of one-half lemon or lime

PREHEAT OVEN TO 350 DEGREES. Thaw frozen pie shell for about
ten minutes. Then, using a fork, poke holes in the pie shell so the
shell won't buckle while it's cooking; set aside. Mix remaining ingredients until smooth and pour into pie shell. Bake 20 minutes, until
the crust is golden brown. Cool on a wire rack then refrigerate until
chilled. You may want to garnish with a dollop of whipped cream.

Serves 6 to 8.

Week 37

This first recipe tastes great just the way it is, but it can also lend itself to exciting adaptations. After you've made it once, see what you think would make it taste even better. Maybe you'll want to throw in some canned mushrooms or frozen peas. Whatever you want to do to make it yours, go ahead and do it! Then you can replace Sherry's name with your own on the recipe.

Sherry's Hamburger Crumble ☆☆☆☆☆

1	pound ground meat (beef, chicken, or turkey)
	Salt, to taste
	Black pepper, to taste
¼	cup flour
1½	cups milk
½	cup water
1	recipe Mashed Potatoes (see page 7)

BROWN THE MEAT IN A FRYING PAN. Pour off excess grease, but not down the sink! Add the salt, pepper, flour, milk, and water, and mix well. Heat the mixture over medium-high heat until the gravy bubbles. Serve over Mashed Potatoes.

Serves 4.

Summer Rosemary Vegetables ☆☆☆☆☆

2	cups sliced carrots
6	tablespoons (¾ stick) butter
1	medium onion, diced

2   (14.5-ounce) cans green beans
1   teaspoon dried rosemary
½   teaspoon garlic salt
    Salt, to taste
    Pepper, to taste

COOK THE CARROTS IN A SMALL AMOUNT of water over medium-high heat until they are tender; drain off water and set aside. Melt the butter in a frying pan over medium-high heat and then sauté the onions until tender. Add cooked carrots, beans, rosemary, garlic salt, salt, and pepper and cook until the beans are warm.

Serves 4 to 6.

Hearts of Palm Salad ☆☆☆☆☆

1   (14-ounce) can hearts of palm (in the international foods
        section or canned vegetables section)
1   green bell pepper, sliced
1   red bell pepper, sliced
1   yellow or orange bell pepper, sliced
1   purple onion, sliced
1   (8-ounce) bottle Italian or Caesar salad dressing
    Salad greens (optional)

DRAIN THE HEARTS OF PALM and cut the stalks into thin circles. Put the peppers, onion, and hearts of palm in a bowl. Cover with salad dressing. Refrigerate until chilled. If desired, serve over salad greens.

Serves 4 to 6.

Week 38

This first recipe comes in handy for either breakfast or lunch. It is easy to fix and takes just a few ingredients. Plus, you can improvise and use the ingredients you have on hand. The tasty Jell-O salad recipe is one of the few in this book that uses Cool Whip, which is never part of a sophisticated menu but will sometimes save you in a pinch.

Fried Egg Sandwich ☆☆☆☆☆

1   egg
1   tablespoon butter, oil, or bacon grease
2   slices bread or 1 English muffin, split
1   slice ham (optional)
1   slice cheese (optional)

FIRST WE NEED TO TEACH YOU how to fry an egg. There are three ways to cook eggs—sunny-side up, over easy, or over hard. Sunny-side up means the egg has never been turned over and the yolk will still be runny. Over easy means that you turn the egg over with a spatula in the process of cooking, being careful not to break the yolk, and brown it for a moment on the other side. Over hard means you turn the egg over and then keep cooking until the yolk is no longer runny in the middle.

Melt the butter or heat the oil over medium heat in a large frying pan. Break the egg by striking the center of the egg on the edge of the pan, just hard enough to break the shell—but not hard enough to smash it. Pull the halves of the shell apart and allow the egg to drop into the pan. Remove any stray shell pieces with a spoon. Reduce the heat to low and continue cooking. Any excess liquid in the pan can be spooned over the top of the egg to hasten the cooking. The egg is done when the whites are no longer runny. You can test that by putting a knife into the white about a quarter inch from the yolk. If the knife comes out clean, the whites are done.

If you're going to make a sandwich, you probably want to cook the egg over hard. When the egg is cooked, place a slice of ham and a slice of cheese on top of the egg in the frying pan. Cook until the ham is warm and the cheese starts to melt. Place the whole stack between two slices of bread or on a split English muffin. You may want to moisten the sandwich with butter or mayonnaise.

Serves 1.

Speedy Jell-O Salad ☆☆☆☆☆

1   (11-ounce) can mandarin oranges, drained
2   cups fresh strawberries or other fruit, cleaned and cut into bite-sized pieces
½   cup chopped pecans
1   (16-ounce) tub Cool Whip®, thawed
1   (6-ounce) package Jell-O®, any flavor

FOLD ORANGES, STRAWBERRIES, and pecans into the Cool Whip in a large bowl. Stir in Jell-O until well combined. Chill until ready to serve.

Serves 6 to 8.

Week 39

Here are some more breakfast treasures—including an egg casserole that will serve a crowd. If you don't know how to cook bacon, now is the time to learn. And you can do tasty things with canned biscuits.

Bacon and Egg Casserole ☆☆☆☆☆

1   pound sliced bacon, diced
1   large onion, chopped
1   (8-ounce) package sliced mushrooms
6   eggs, lightly beaten
4   cups frozen shredded hash brown potatoes, thawed
2   cups shredded cheddar cheese
1½ cups cottage cheese
1¼ cups shredded Swiss cheese

PREHEAT OVEN TO 350 DEGREES. In large skillet, cook the bacon, onion, and mushrooms over medium-high heat until the bacon is crisp and the vegetables are limp. Drain off the excess juice and grease into a can you'll throw away. In a large bowl, mix together the eggs, hash browns, and cheeses. Add the bacon mixture to the egg mixture. Pour into a greased 9x13-inch baking pan. Bake, uncovered, for 35 to 40 minutes, or until the eggs are set and bubbly. Take the dish out of the oven and let it sit 10 minutes before serving.

Serves 8 to 10.

Biscuit Treasures ☆☆☆☆☆

1   can refrigerated biscuit dough
    Butter
    Cinnamon
    Sugar
    Jam or jelly (optional)

TAKE THE BISCUITS OUT of the cardboard tube. (If you've never opened one of these tubes before, there are instructions on the side of the can.) Separate and flatten each biscuit individually on a cutting board, using your hand, a rolling pin, or the side of a straight drinking glass. In the center of each biscuit put a small dollop (about a measuring teaspoon) of butter. On top of that, put a teaspoon of sugar, followed by a sprinkling of cinnamon. If you prefer, you can use a teaspoon of jam or jelly instead of the sugar and cinnamon. Tightly pinch together the edges of the biscuits so that the filling won't leak out. Put the biscuit pouches on a cookie sheet and bake according to the directions on the biscuit can.

Serves 4 to 6.

Week 40

It's soup season again, and taco soup is a particular favorite. Here is a soup with a crunchy surprise at the bottom that is sure to make it one of your favorite soup recipes. If you can't find cans exactly the same size as what's specified in the recipe, just use what you can find. Remember— cooking is an art, not a science.

Kathy's Taco Soup ☆☆☆☆☆

1	pound ground meat (beef, turkey, chicken)
1	large onion, chopped
3	(15.5-ounce) cans red beans, undrained
1	(15-ounce) can whole kernel corn, undrained
1	(15-ounce) can tomato sauce
1	(14.5-ounce) can diced spicy tomatoes (Rotel is an excellent brand), undrained
2	(4.5-ounce) cans chopped green chilies
1 to 2	(1.25-ounce) envelopes taco seasoning mix
¼	teaspoon red pepper flakes
1½	cups water
1	(15-ounce) bag Fritos®
	Shredded cheddar cheese, for topping

SAUTÉ MEAT AND ONIONS in a large pot over medium-high heat until the meat is no longer pink and the onions are translucent, stirring until the meat crumbles. Drain off fat if necessary. Stir everything except the Fritos and cheese into the meat mixture; bring to a boil. Reduce heat and simmer, uncovered, for 15 minutes, stirring occasionally.

To serve, throw a big handful of Fritos in each bowl. Pour the soup over the Fritos. Top with shredded cheddar cheese, or whatever else strikes your fancy.

Serves 4 to 6.

Mexican Salad ☆☆☆☆☆

1	bag mixed salad greens
1	(10-ounce) box frozen corn, thawed
2	large tomatoes, chopped
3 to 4	green onions, chopped
1	cup canned black beans, rinsed and drained
1	cup mayonnaise
1	(16-ounce) bottle salsa
	Shredded cheddar or Monterey Jack cheese, for topping

IN A LARGE BOWL, TOSS THE SALAD GREENS with corn, tomatoes, green onions, and beans. In a separate bowl, mix the mayonnaise and salsa to make a dressing. Pour dressing over salad, sprinkle with cheese, and serve.

Serves 4 to 6.

Susie's Turtle Cake ☆☆☆☆☆

1 box German chocolate cake mix, mixed according to directions on box but not yet baked

48 Kraft® caramels (1 14-ounce bag)

½ cup evaporated milk

2 cups pecans, chopped

¾ cup (1½ sticks) butter (not margarine!)

2 cups semi-sweet chocolate chips

Whipped cream, for topping

GREASE AND FLOUR A 9X13-INCH PAN. Preheat oven to 350 degrees. Pour half of the cake batter into the prepared pan. Bake 15 minutes. While the cake is baking, melt the caramels, milk, and butter in a large saucepan over medium heat. Pour the mixture over the partially baked cake. Sprinkle half of the pecans and half of the chocolate chips over the caramel mixture. Pour the rest of the batter over that. Sprinkle the rest of the nuts and chocolate chips on top. Bake 20 more minutes. It won't look quite done when it's finished, but it will firm up when it sets. (It tastes better the second day!) Serve topped with whipped cream.

Serves 12 to 16.

Week 41

Here's another soup recipe for you, and it might just be the best mine-strone soup on the planet. Don't let the number of ingredients intimidate you—almost everything is in a can. If you can find the courage to make this once, it is going to be one of your favorite recipes. And it makes a big enough pot of soup that you'll be able to eat ten or twelve bowls of it. Don't leave out the fennel seeds, even if you've never heard of fennel. Fennel is what makes this recipe so good.

Kathy's Hearty Minestrone ☆☆☆☆☆

1	pound Polish sausage (hot or mild)
2	tablespoons olive oil
1	large onion, chopped
4	large cloves garlic, chopped
4	(14-ounce) cans chicken broth
1	(28-ounce) can diced tomatoes
1	(10-ounce) box chopped frozen spinach (make sure it's chopped!)
1½	cups sliced carrots
2	teaspoons dried basil
1	teaspoon dried oregano
2	teaspoons fennel seeds
½	teaspoon red pepper flakes
1	(19-ounce) can red beans
1	cup small dried pasta (shells, if you can find them)

1   (10-ounce) package frozen cut green beans
    Grated Parmesan cheese, for topping

PIERCE THE SKINS OF THE SAUSAGES with a fork; place them in a saucepan and cover with water. Bring to a boil, then cover and let simmer for 15 minutes or until cooked. Drain the liquid into a separate bowl. When the sausages are cool enough to touch, cut them into small slices.

In a large pot over medium-high heat, lightly brown the sausage slices in hot olive oil. Add the onions and the garlic, and cook until the onions are softened. Add the chicken broth, diced tomatoes (including liquid), frozen spinach, carrots, basil, oregano, fennel seeds, and red pepper flakes. Bring mixture to a boil; reduce the heat and let it simmer, covered, for 10 minutes, or until the vegetables are almost tender.

Add the red beans (including liquid), the pasta, and the frozen beans. Let mixture simmer 5 to 7 minutes more, or until the pasta is tender but firm. Season the soup to taste. (It can be thinned with additional chicken broth or with the water from boiling the sausages, if necessary.) Serve topped with grated Parmesan cheese.

Serves 10 to 12.

Gold and Red Apple Salad ☆☆☆☆☆

1   large Golden Delicious apple, cored and chopped

1   large Red Delicious apple, cored and chopped

2   teaspoons lemon juice

1   (20-ounce) can pineapple chunks, drained

1   cup miniature marshmallows

⅔   cup flaked coconut

½   cup chopped pecans

¼   cup Craisins®

¼   cup mayonnaise

1   stalk celery, thinly sliced

IN A LARGE BOWL, TOSS THE APPLES with the lemon juice. Add the remaining ingredients and mix well. Cover and chill for at least 1 hour before serving.

Serves 6 to 8.

Week 42

When it's cold outside, sometimes you want a casual dinner that will warm you up and bring a smile to your face. Lucky for you, Joe's Sloppy Joes and Mexican Chowder couldn't be easier to make.

Joe's Sloppy Joes ☆☆☆☆☆

1	pound lean ground meat (beef, turkey, or chicken)
1	large onion, chopped
¼	cup ketchup
1	teaspoon mustard
1	(10.75-ounce) can chicken gumbo soup
1	teaspoon Worcestershire sauce
1	teaspoon dried sage
1	teaspoon salt
1	teaspoon brown sugar
4 to 6	hamburger buns

BROWN THE GROUND MEAT AND THE ONION in a skillet over medium-high heat, until the meat is cooked and the onions are clear. Stir in ketchup, mustard, chicken gumbo soup, Worcestershire sauce, sage, salt, and brown sugar; combine well. Cover the pan and cook over low heat for 45 minutes, stirring occasionally. Serve on hamburger buns.

Serves 4 to 6.

Mexican Chowder ☆☆☆☆☆

1   pound ground meat (beef, chicken, or turkey)
2   tablespoons vegetable oil
1   envelope French's® Chili-O seasoning mix
2⅔ cups cold water
1   (14.5-ounce) can diced tomatoes, with liquid
1   (15.5-ounce) can red kidney beans, with liquid
1   cup small macaroni noodles
1   (16-ounce) can corn, with liquid
    Grated cheddar cheese, for topping

BROWN THE MEAT in the vegetable oil in a large skillet. Add the Chili-O mix, water, tomatoes, and beans. Bring the mixture to a boil, then add the macaroni and cook for another 10 minutes, until the macaroni is tender. Add corn and heat again until the corn is warm. Serve hot, topped with cheese.

Serves 4.

Week 43

You've probably eaten fettuccine in restaurants lots of times, but you may not have realized it was this easy to make. Once you've mastered the basic recipe, you can customize it by adding mushrooms, frozen peas, cooked shrimp, or whatever else sounds good to you. It's your recipe. Don't hesitate to make it your own. You can complement the fettuccine with a cool salad and finish everything off with an ice cream pie.

Fettuccine ☆☆☆☆☆

1   (16-ounce) package fettuccine noodles
½   cup (1 stick) butter
2   tablespoons flour
½   cup milk
¼   cup grated Parmesan or mozzarella cheese
   Black pepper (optional)

COOK THE NOODLES ACCORDING TO package directions. While the noodles are boiling, melt the butter on low heat in a saucepan. Add the flour, and stir together to form a thin paste. Cook and stir for about 1 minute, until the mixture turns a light, nutty color. Add the milk slowly and keep cooking and stirring until the mixture thickens and coats the back of a spoon.

Butter the insides of a large dish; pour the noodles into the dish. The butter adds flavor and keeps the noodles from sticking. Add the white sauce you just made, the Parmesan cheese, and black pepper, to taste. This should be creamy—not runny or stiff. If it's too stiff, add a little warm milk and stir everything together.

See Appendix A for instructions on cooking pasta.
Serves 4 to 6.

Antipasto Salad ☆☆☆☆☆

1   large head lettuce, cut into 8 wedges
1   bottle Caesar or Italian salad dressing
    Any six of the following ingredients:
1   (6-ounce) can black olives, drained
1   (10-ounce) bottle marinated artichoke hearts
3   hard-boiled eggs, sliced
2   large tomatoes, cut into wedges
1   green pepper, cut into rings
¼   pound sliced provolone cheese
¼   pound thinly sliced pepperoni or salami
1   cucumber, peeled and sliced
12   rolled anchovies
1   tablespoon capers

ARRANGE EVERYTHING BUT THE DRESSING nicely on a platter and let people serve themselves. Serve the dressing on the side.

Serves 8.

Ice Cream Sundae Pie ☆☆☆☆☆

1   graham cracker pie crust (buy it pre-made at the grocery
    store)
4   cups ice cream, slightly softened, any flavor
1   cup ice cream topping (fudge sauce, caramel, or
    butterscotch)
    Whipped cream, for topping
    Nuts, for topping
    Maraschino cherries, for topping

PLACE A THIN LAYER OF ICE CREAM on top of the pie crust; cover it with a thin layer of ice cream topping. Continue alternating layers of softened ice cream and topping. Cover the pie with foil or plastic wrap and place it in the freezer. Freeze until the pie is firm, at least four or five hours. To serve, slice it into wedges and top with whipped cream, nuts, cherries, and extra topping.

Serves 6 to 8.

Week 44

Soup is one of the most satisfying meals you can make, and it doesn't have to be hard. All of the soup recipes in this book are easy, but this one can be done by anyone who can brown a pound of ground meat. Serve it with Cheesy Cornbread and you have a winning combination.

Almost Instant Soup ☆☆☆☆☆

Vegetable oil
1 pound ground meat (beef, turkey, or chicken)
1 large onion, chopped
3 to 4 red or white potatoes, scrubbed and chopped
1 (16-ounce) bag frozen peas and carrots
1 (14.5-ounce) can green beans
1 (10.75-ounce) can tomato soup
1 (15.25-ounce) can corn
2 (14.5-ounce) cans chopped, stewed tomatoes
Salt, pepper, and garlic powder, to taste

HEAT A SMALL AMOUNT OF VEGETABLE OIL in a large pot. Add ground meat and onion and cook over medium-high heat until meat is browned and onion is tender. Add the remaining ingredients, including the liquid in the cans of vegetables, except for the seasonings. Cook the mixture for about five minutes over medium heat. Add the seasonings to taste. (Yes, it's okay to taste the food while it's cooking!) Cover, and cook for another 30 minutes. In addition to the seasonings mentioned above, you might want to try chili powder, cayenne pepper, or even a little nutmeg. Let your taste buds be your guide!

Serves 8 to 12.

Cheesy Cornbread ☆☆☆☆☆

1   egg
¾   cup milk
2   tablespoons vegetable oil
¾   cup flour
2½ teaspoons baking powder
¾   teaspoon salt
1   tablespoon sugar
½   cup yellow cornmeal
1   cup shredded cheddar cheese

PREHEAT OVEN TO 400 DEGREES. In a mixing bowl, beat the egg, then add the milk and vegetable oil. In another bowl, combine the flour, baking powder, salt, and sugar. Stir in the cornmeal and shredded cheese to the dry mixture. Add the dry mixture to the wet mixture and stir until the dry ingredients are just barely wet. Grease an 8x8-inch glass baking pan and pour the batter into the pan. Bake 20 to 25 minutes, or until lightly browned on top.

Serves 9.

Week 45

If you're looking for some warm food on a cold night, these recipes are easy to fix and will stick to your ribs. After you've made the first recipe once, you can vary it by adding other ingredients (such as frozen peas or sliced and sautéed mushrooms) to the recipe. There aren't any rules here; feel free to experiment!

Ham and Potatoes Au Gratin ☆☆☆☆☆

¼   cup (½ stick) butter

1   onion, diced

3   tablespoons flour

2   cups milk

    Salt, to taste

    Black pepper, to taste

1½   cups cooked ham, diced

3   large red or white potatoes, washed, scrubbed and diced

½   cup grated cheddar cheese

3   tablespoons dry bread crumbs

PREHEAT OVEN TO 400 DEGREES. You can buy commercial containers of bread crumbs, or you can make your own by crumbling half a slice of stale or toasted bread by hand. Melt the butter in a large skillet over medium heat. Add the onion and sauté until onion is softened. Blend in the flour and stir for a minute or two until the mixture turns a nice nutty-brown color. Gradually add the milk and cook over medium heat, stirring until thickened. Add the salt and pepper. Combine the ham and potatoes in a casserole dish, then pour the sauce you made over them. Sprinkle cheese and bread crumbs over top. Bake for 20 minutes, until golden brown and bubbly.

Serves 4 to 6.

Spinach Salad ☆☆☆☆☆

1 bag spinach greens
3 hard-boiled eggs, sliced
1 cup croutons
1 (15-ounce) can mandarin orange slices, drained
1 bottled Caesar salad dressing or Italian dressing
¼ cup bacon bits (available in bottles in the grocery store)

CHECK THE BAG OF SPINACH LEAVES to make sure they have been washed. If they are not clean, rinse them off well and pat the leaves dry with several paper towels. Put the leaves in a salad bowl and add the other ingredients except for the dressing. If you have any frozen peas available, feel free to throw in a few without even bothering to cook them. Stir or toss the salad to blend the ingredients. Pour the dressing on top of the salad just before serving.

Serves 4 to 6.

Cherry Crisp ☆☆☆☆☆

2 (21-ounce) cans cherry pie filling
1 box yellow cake mix
1¾ cups chopped pecans
1 cup (2 sticks) butter, melted

PREHEAT OVEN TO 350 DEGREES. Pour the pie filling into the bottom of a 9x13-inch glass baking dish. Sprinkle the cake mix over the top but do not stir. Top with the chopped pecans, then pour the melted butter on top of that. Bake for about 30 minutes. Cool and then serve. Optionally, top with some vanilla ice cream or freshly whipped cream.

Serves 6 to 8.

Week 46

If you wind up having to cook Thanksgiving dinner, do not panic! A turkey dinner is not that difficult to prepare. Supplement the turkey and dressing with some of the other recipes in this book. Mashed potatoes, gravy, fried corn, and Thanksgiving salad round out a good Thanksgiving dinner. See Appendix A for instructions for how to bake a turkey and how to make pan gravy.

Turkey Dressing (Stuffing) ☆☆☆☆☆

1   loaf bread (or a pan of unsweetened cornbread)
¼   cup (½ stick) butter
1   cup chopped celery (approximate)
1   large onion, chopped
2   teaspoons poultry seasoning
1   (14-ounce) can chicken broth, heated
    Salt, to taste
    Black pepper to taste

BREAK THE BREAD INTO BITE-SIZED PIECES (or crumble the cornbread); set aside. Melt the butter in a large pot over medium heat. Add the celery and onion and cook over low heat until the vegetables are no longer crunchy. Turn off the heat. Add the bread and stir well. Sprinkle some poultry seasoning on top and mix again. Pour hot chicken broth over the top until the bread is moistened. You may not need the whole can. Add salt and pepper to taste. Cover until it's time to serve, so the steam will keep the dressing moist.

Serves 8 to 10.

Thanksgiving Salad ☆☆☆☆☆

1   bag mixed salad greens
½   cup Craisins® (dried cranberries)
1   (11-ounce) can mandarin oranges, drained
½   cup chopped or sliced almonds (or pine nuts)
    Bottled Italian or Caesar salad dressing
    Croutons (optional)

COMBINE SALAD GREENS, Craisins, mandarin oranges, and almonds in a large bowl. To serve, toss with a little dressing and top with croutons, if using.

Serves 4 to 6.

Oven-Roasted Potatoes ☆☆☆☆☆

2   pounds red or white potatoes, scrubbed and cut into bite-sized chunks
1   (1-ounce) envelope onion soup mix
⅓   cup vegetable oil
    One large plastic zipper bag

PREHEAT OVEN TO 400 DEGREES. Put potatoes, soup mix, and oil in the plastic bag. Close the bag and shake until all potatoes are well coated. Pour contents of bag into a 9x13-inch baking dish or a 2-quart casserole dish. Bake until potatoes are soft when pierced by a fork (an hour or less, check at 30 minutes). Potatoes will be golden brown.

Serves 4 to 6.

Week 47

If you're lucky enough to have some leftover Thanksgiving turkey, this is a great way to use the leftovers. If not, you can use cooked chicken instead.

Turkey and Biscuits ☆☆☆☆☆

1   can refrigerator biscuits
1   onion, chopped
    Vegetable oil
2   cups cooked, chopped turkey (approximately)
2   (10.75-ounce) cans cream of chicken soup
½   soup can of water
1   (16-ounce) bag frozen peas and carrots, thawed

BAKE THE BISCUITS according to the directions on the package. Sauté the onion in a frying pan over medium heat with a little bit of vegetable oil until the onion is no longer crunchy. Add the turkey and soup and enough water that the soup starts to look like gravy (start with about half a soup can and go from there). Cook over low heat, stirring to remove the lumps in the soup. When the mixture is hot and bubbly, add the formerly frozen vegetables. Add salt and pepper to taste.

Put two biscuits in the bottom of each serving bowl (or plate) and pour the turkey mixture over them.

Serves 2 to 4.

Poultry Stir-Fry ☆☆☆☆☆

1   (16-ounce) package frozen vegetables, thawed
2   cups cooked, chopped turkey or chicken
1   cup bottled teriyaki sauce
2   tablespoons soy sauce
1   cup cooked spaghetti noodles

SELECT A VARIETY OF FROZEN VEGETABLES that will make for a tasty stir-fry. Many stores offer vegetable blends such as stir-fry blend, soup blend, or mixed vegetable blend. If you cannot find a blend that sounds good, you can buy individual frozen vegetables such as broccoli, cauliflower, baby corn, carrots, celery, water chestnuts, and sugar peas and use those instead.

Place the turkey in a bowl with the teriyaki sauce. Allow the meat to marinate in the sauce for at least one hour. Pour the mixture into a hot skillet and cook the meat until it is slightly brown on the outside. Stir in the thawed vegetables and the soy sauce. Turn the heat up to high and stir the mixture constantly for 5 minutes. Reduce heat to low and let the mixture simmer for 10 minutes. Stir in the cooked spaghetti noodles and let the mixture simmer for an additional 5 minutes. Add just a little more teriyaki sauce, and stir it in. Cool slightly and then serve.

As a variation, serve the mixture on top of rice instead of stirring in the noodles. You can find instructions in Appendix A for cooking both rice and pasta.

Serves 4 to 6.

Week 48

The first recipe for this week works equally well with turkey, if you still have some leftovers. There is also an option provided for turning it into beef stew.

Kathy's Chicken Stew ☆☆☆☆☆

1	tablespoon vegetable oil
12	cups boiling water
4	onions, sliced
4	teaspoons Worcestershire sauce
6	bay leaves
3	tablespoons salt
1	teaspoon black pepper
	Dash cayenne pepper
2	teaspoons paprika
¼	teaspoon allspice
1	tablespoon sugar
12	carrots cut into 1-inch pieces
8	large red or white potatoes, cubed
4	cups fresh mushrooms, cleaned and cut in half
⅛	cup flour
¾	cup cold water
3	pounds boneless, skinless chicken breasts, cooked and cubed
2	(10-ounce) boxes frozen peas

PLACE THE VEGETABLE OIL, BOILING WATER, sliced onion, Worcestershire sauce, and all of the seasonings in a large soup pot. Cover the pot and simmer for 1 hour. Add the carrots and potatoes. Cook uncovered over medium heat until the vegetables are half done (about five minutes). Stir in the mushrooms and continue cooking uncovered until vegetables are done (about five more minutes).

Combine the flour and water in a jar with a leak-proof top. Put on the top and shake the flour and water mixture vigorously until the flour is evenly mixed. Open the jar and pour the mixture into the stew pan slowly, stirring as you add it. Continue to cook and stir the stew over medium heat until the liquid reaches the consistency of gravy. See Appendix A for complete details about making pan gravy.

Add the chicken and cook until meat is heated through. Taste the stew before it's done cooking. This stew is supposed to have a bite to it. If it tastes bland, add more paprika and allspice until it has some flavor. Add the peas just before serving.

If you prefer an old-fashioned beef stew, put 2 pounds trimmed stew meat and the juice from 2 lemons in the water when you begin to simmer the spices; simmer for 3 hours (instead of 1), or until the beef is tender.

Serves 6 to 10.

Cheddar Biscuits ☆☆☆☆☆

- 2 cups Bisquick® mix
- ½ cup cold milk
- ¾ cup grated cheddar cheese
- ¼ cup (½ stick) butter
- 1 teaspoon dried parsley flakes
- ½ teaspoon garlic powder
- ½ teaspoon dried Italian seasoning

PREHEAT OVEN TO 450 DEGREES. Use a fork to combine the Bisquick mix and the milk in a large bowl until the lumps are gone and there are no dry pockets. Add the cheese and blend well. Drop tablespoon-sized mounds of dough onto a cookie sheet. Bake 8 to 10 minutes.

While the biscuits are baking, melt the butter in the microwave in a small bowl. Stir in the spices. When the biscuits come out of the oven, brush the tops with the butter and spices. Serve immediately.

Makes 1 dozen biscuits.

Week 49

Right now is the perfect time to take advantage of the cranberries that are fresh in the grocery store. But you can make this chicken treat all year round by using canned cranberries if no fresh ones are available. You can also buy an extra bag of fresh cranberries now and freeze it to use later.

Shannon's Cranberry Chicken ☆☆☆☆☆

- 8 boneless, skinless chicken breasts
- 1 teaspoon vegetable oil
- ¾ cup thinly sliced onion
- 1 cup ketchup
- ½ cup brown sugar
- 1½ tablespoons vinegar
- 1½ teaspoons dry mustard (in the spice aisle)
- 2 cups cranberries, fresh or frozen (thawed) or 1 (16-ounce) can whole cranberries

PREHEAT OVEN TO 400 DEGREES. Spray or butter a 9x13-inch baking dish; set aside. Arrange chicken in the baking dish. Bake for 25 minutes, uncovered. While the chicken cooks, heat the oil in a nonstick skillet over medium heat. Add onions and cook until softened. Turn off the heat and stir in the other ingredients. Remove the chicken after 25 minutes and spoon the cranberry sauce over it. Return it to the oven and bake for an additional 10 to 15 minutes or until the chicken is done.

Serves 8.

Apple Cobbler Cake ☆☆☆☆☆

2 (16-ounce) cans apple pie filling (or blackberry or peach)
1 package yellow cake mix
¾ cup (1½ sticks) butter, softened
⅔ cup chopped pecans
½ teaspoon cinnamon
½ cup milk
  Whipped cream or vanilla ice cream, for topping

PREHEAT OVEN TO 375 DEGREES. Heat the pie filling in a saucepan over medium heat until it's just beginning to bubble, stirring occasionally. Meanwhile, combine cake mix and butter in a large bowl and blend at low speed with an electric mixer (or use a fork or wire whisk if you don't have a mixer) until crumbly.

Place 1½ cups of the cake mixture in a medium bowl. Add the nuts and cinnamon and stir until well mixed; set aside.

Add milk to the remaining cake mixture in the large bowl and stir until moistened. Spoon the hot pie filling into an ungreased, 9x13-inch baking pan. Top with heaping spoonfuls of the batter from the large bowl. Sprinkle with the topping. Bake 30 to 40 minutes, or until golden brown. Cool 30 minutes, and serve warm with ice cream or whipped cream.

Serves 8 to 12.

Week 50

This week's menu is the reason many cooks have multiple rectangular glass baking dishes. You can never go wrong with glass baking dishes! They're easy to clean, and there's no non-stick surface to come off in your food. Just don't use them in the broiler.

Oriental Honey Salmon ☆☆☆☆☆

⅓ cup honey

3 tablespoons soy sauce

2 tablespoons lemon juice

1 tablespoon Dijon mustard

4 (6-ounce) pieces salmon

IN A SMALL MIXING BOWL, combine all the liquid ingredients and mix with a wire whisk or fork. Place the salmon pieces in a small glass baking dish, and pour about a third of the sauce over the fish. Turn each salmon piece over in the dish, so that the sauce will cover both sides. Place the dish in the refrigerator for at least two hours so the sauce will flavor the fish.

Butter the bottom of a frying pan or spray it with cooking spray. Cook the salmon over medium heat for 4 to 6 minutes on each side, until the meat is golden and cooked through when you cut it with a fork. Remove the meat from the frying pan and add the remaining sauce to the pan. Cook mixture over low heat, stirring until the sauce comes to a boil. Return the salmon to the pan, heat for a few more minutes, and then serve immediately.

Serves 4.

Easy Potato Casserole ☆☆☆☆☆

2 (1-pound) packages shredded potatoes

2 (10.75-ounce) cans cream of potato soup

1 pint sour cream

¼ teaspoon garlic powder

Salt, to taste

Black pepper, to taste

2 cups grated cheddar cheese

PREHEAT OVEN TO 350 DEGREES. If you are using frozen potatoes instead of ones from the refrigerator section of the store, make sure you thaw them first. Combine all ingredients except the cheese in a 9x13-inch rectangular baking dish and mix well. Sprinkle the cheese on top. Bake for 1 hour, until hot and bubbly.

Serves 6 to 8.

Week 51

This is the time of year when your refrigerator might be filled with leftover chicken or turkey, so we'll pass along another great recipe for getting rid of it. Don't be afraid to experiment by adding thawed frozen peas, chopped green onions, or even a little cranberry sauce.

Chicken Rolls ☆☆☆☆☆

1	can refrigerated crescent dinner rolls
2	cups cooked, cubed chicken
1½	cups grated cheddar cheese
1	(10.75-ounce) can cream of chicken soup
½	soup can milk

PREHEAT OVEN TO 350 DEGREES. Open the tube of crescent rolls, and separate and unroll each triangular-shaped roll. Put some chopped chicken on the wide end of each roll, and top with a tablespoon or two of grated cheese. Roll the dough up, starting with chicken end. Fold each end of the roll over so that the chicken doesn't fall out. Mix the soup and the milk together in a small bowl, stirring until smooth. Pour enough of the soup mixture on in a rectangular baking dish to just cover the bottom. Put the chicken rolls in the pan. Pour the rest of the soup mixture on top. Sprinkle more grated cheese over the whole thing and bake 35 minutes.

Serves 4 to 6.

Cranberry Pie ☆☆☆☆☆

½ cup (1 stick) butter
¼ cup shortening
2½ cups fresh cranberries
1½ cups sugar, divided
½ cup chopped pecans
1 teaspoon orange zest (grated orange peel)
2 eggs
1 cup flour

MELT THE BUTTER AND SHORTENING in a small saucepan over low heat; set aside to cool. Preheat oven to 325 degrees. Butter a 9-inch glass pie plate.

Spread the cranberries evenly over the bottom of the pie plate. Sprinkle with ½ cup of the sugar, the pecans, and the orange zest. Set aside. Beat the eggs in a mixing bowl, and then stir in the flour, the butter/shortening mixture, and the remaining 1 cup of sugar. Mix well, and pour over the cranberries. Bake for about an hour, until the crust is nicely browned. Serve plain or topped with whipped cream or ice cream.

Serves 6 to 8.

Week 52

You may be thinking of having guests over for New Year's Eve. If you want to serve them a proper supper, ham is a good way to begin. Canned yams are an easy accompaniment, and Cheesecake Cupcakes make for a tasty dessert. Now you can ring in the New Year in style!

Baked Ham ☆☆☆☆☆

- 1 ready-to-serve ham (canned or refrigerated)
- ¼ cup Dijon mustard
- ¼ cup brown sugar, packed
- 1 (16-ounce) can pineapple slices
- 2 cups apple juice

PUT THE HAM IN A ROASTING PAN and use a sharp knife to make diamond-shaped cuts all over the top of the ham. Heat according to the package directions, and then remove pan from the oven. Mix the mustard and sugar into a paste, and rub it all over the outside of the ham. Put the pineapple slices on the ham—you may have to stick them on with toothpicks for now. Pour the apple juice over the ham and in the pan. Put the ham in a 325-degree oven for fifteen minutes or so, allowing the toppings to blend with the ham but not burn. Remove toothpicks and serve.

Cheesecake Cupcakes ☆☆☆☆☆

12   pieces Nestlé® refrigerated chocolate chip or sugar cookie
       dough
1   (8-ounce) package cream cheese, room temperature
½   cup sweetened condensed milk
1   teaspoon vanilla
1   (21-ounce) can cherry pie filling
       Paper cupcake liners

PREHEAT OVEN TO 325 DEGREES. If you have a muffin pan, fill it
with paper cupcake liners. If you don't, put the muffin liners together
in a square baking dish (you may be able to bake only nine at a time).
Put one piece of cookie dough in each muffin liner. Bake 10 to 12
minutes, so the cookie dough expands to the edges of the liners.
Remove from oven.

Beat cream cheese, condensed milk, and vanilla in a medium bowl
until smooth. Put about 3 tablespoons of this mixture into each cupcake. Bake for another 15 to 18 minutes, until set. Cool completely
in pan. Top each with a tablespoon of pie filling. Refrigerate 1 hour
before serving.

Makes 12 cheesecakes.

Appendix A
Common Cooking Procedures

There are many procedures that experienced cooks may know but that you may not. If any of our recipes contain instructions that might be unclear to a novice cook, we have tried to explain them here so that you will soon be an expert.

How to Bake Potatoes

Choose brown "baking potatoes" for baking. These are typically called russet potatoes. Choose potatoes that do not have any bad spots on them. Always scrub the potatoes well to get off the dirt. This is especially important if you plan on eating the skin, which is the healthiest part of the potato. Rub each potato with a little bit of vegetable oil to keep the skins tender. Punch holes in each potato with a fork to keep them from exploding in the oven. Bake them on the oven rack at about 425 degrees. An hour should do for all but the biggest potatoes, but you can test for doneness by sticking a knife or a fork into them. Potatoes are done when the fork or knife slides in without resistance.

How to Boil Eggs

Put the eggs in a saucepan. Put enough water in the saucepan to cover the eggs by about an inch. Turn on the heat and bring the water to a boil (that's when the water is bubbling). Continue to cook the eggs for 3 minutes more for soft-boiled eggs or 10 minutes more for hard-boiled eggs. (At higher altitudes, eggs will take longer to boil.) Remove from heat. Carefully drain the hot water off the eggs. Put the pan in the sink and run cold water over the eggs. (This will shrink the eggs inside the shells so they are easier to peel.) If you have hard-boiled your eggs, you can drain the cold water from the pan and bounce the egg around until the shell is completely cracked. Then just wash off the peel and the eggs are ready to eat.

How to Boil Water/How to Cook Noodles

If you've never cooked noodles, do not despair! This basic task is so easy that once you've done it you'll be a pro for the rest of your life. Put a big pot of water on the burner. You'll probably want about 4 quarts (that's 16 cups) to cook a pound of pasta. Throw in a little salt (a teaspoon should do it, but you don't have to measure). Bring the water to a boil (water is boiling when big bubbles come up from the bottom and break the surface of the water). Add noodles. Stir. Bring water to a boil again. Then start the timer and cook the length of time that is directed on the package. If the water threatens to boil over, add a little bit of cooking oil to the water to calm it. If that doesn't help, you'll have to scoop out the excess water—taking care not to burn yourself in the process.

Noodles are done when they taste done. They should be just slightly firm to the teeth (that's called *al dente* in Italian) and not too mushy. When they're done, immediately take them from the heat and drain them in a colander that's in the kitchen sink. Shake the colander to get the water out and then return the noodles to the hot pot. This will help any excess water to evaporate.

How to Brown Ground Beef

Browning ground beef (or ground chicken or ground turkey) is a basic kitchen skill. First, choose lean or extra lean beef, because regular ground beef will leave you a lot of grease and not a lot of meat. Next, put the meat in a frying pan and cook over medium heat, separating the meat with a spoon or spatula into little pieces. Keep cooking and stirring and separating until the meat loses its pink color. It will still be chewy—do not keep cooking until the meat has turned into little shotgun pellets! If there's any grease, drain it off. The meat is ready to use in your recipe.

How to Buy and Store Avocados

Pick out any avocado in the grocery store. Store at room temperature until the avocado starts to get a little soft when you press on the skin. Then refrigerate until you are ready to use the avocado. Avocados go brown when exposed to air, so eat them quickly after removing the skins or sprinkle them with lemon juice.

How to Cook Bacon

Bacon isn't particularly hard to cook. The biggest challenge is that bacon strips are rectangular and frying pans are round, but until square frying pans are available, this is something we're just going to have to live with. Take as many strips of bacon as you want out of the package and put the rest of the package safely back in the refrigerator. Arrange the strips on the bottom of a frying pan, next to each other but not overlapping. If you have more bacon than pan, you can be creative and start some strips along the sides of the pan. Eventually the bacon will shrink and you can cook it all in the pan. Now turn the heat up to medium and let 'er rip. As the fat starts to melt, make sure the grease doesn't splatter in your eyes. You can hold the bacon down to the surface of the pan by squashing it with a spatula, if you want. When the bacon is brown on one side, turn it over and cook the other side until the bacon is as done as you like. Some people like it crispy, and others don't. It's your choice. Be warned, however, that once the bacon has been turned over it's going to cook awfully fast. Don't let it burn! When the bacon is done according to your taste, turn off the heat and remove the bacon to a bed of paper towels to drain for a couple of minutes.

Do not dispose of the bacon grease down the sink, or you're in for a world of trouble later. Wait until the grease has hardened and then scoop it into a garbage can, or save the bacon grease to use later. Although bacon grease is very unhealthy, it can impart a great flavor to food if used to sauté onions or other vegetables. Be sure to use it sparingly!

You can also bake bacon in the oven. Preheat the oven to 400 degrees. Put the bacon slices on a jelly roll pan or cookie sheet with sides or a broiler pan to catch the fat. Bake 20 minutes, but check after 15. You can cook a whole pound of bacon at once this way.

How to Cook Frozen Vegetables

If you've purchased frozen vegetables that come with a sauce, follow the recipe on the package. If, however, you've purchased plain old frozen vegetables, they're all cooked the same way. This is how to do it. Using a saucepan that's bigger than the amount of vegetables you want to cook, put a little bit of water in the bottom of the pan. The operative phrase here is "little bit," because there's enough water in the frozen vegetables to provide most of the water you'll need. If you're cooking one of those standard boxes of vegetables, about ¼ cup water should be plenty—unless you're cooking lima beans, which need more water and longer cooking times. (By the way, those boxes are just the right size if you're cooking for one or two.) Put the frozen vegetables on top of the water. You don't need to thaw them first, but it would help if you'd break up the vegetables in the box or bag before you dump them into the pan. Heat the vegetables, stirring occasionally, until they are heated through. During the process of cooking, you can flavor the vegetables by adding butter or salt or seasonings. Butter always tastes the best, but face it—if you get in the butter habit you're going to regret it one of these days. Experiment with dried basil or oregano or some of the vegetable seasoning blends that are in the spices area of your supermarket. When the vegetables have cooked, they're ready to serve. Drain off any liquid that is left, and you're ready to eat.

How to Cook Rice

For every 1 cup rice, use 2 cups water. Put rice and water in a pot that has a lid. Add 1 teaspoon salt (optional) and 1 teaspoon butter or oil (also optional). Turn on the heat and bring the water to a boil. Immediately put the lid on the pot and turn the heat down to low. DO NOT PEEK! Cook about 12 minutes for white rice. Remove the pot from the heat WITHOUT REMOVING THE LID, and allow the rice at least five minutes to absorb the water. Uncover, fluff with a fork, and the rice is ready to serve.

Note that brown rice requires about a ¼ cup more water and a substantially longer cooking time. Count on a good 45 minutes of cooking time for brown rice. Make sure you have that heat on low, so the rice doesn't burn!

How to Make a Roux

A roux (pronounced "roo," as in the second half of kanga-) is a mixture of flour and some kind of fat (butter or oil), which is used to thicken soups, sauces, and stews. A roux comes in three varieties: light, dark, and very dark. A light roux cooks only a few minutes and is light in color and flavor. Its primary use is to thicken a soup or white sauce. Many of the recipes in this book use a light roux. Almost every true Cajun recipe begins with the words, "First, you make a roux." A dark roux is the color of fudge and has a rich flavor. A very dark roux (which should probably be prepared by professional chefs only) is sometimes called a brick roux and gains a reddish color after cooking for a long time.

We'll explain here how to make the dark roux that forms the base of so many tempting Cajun dishes. Mix equal parts cooking oil and white flour in a saucepan. Cook over *low* heat, stirring *constantly*, until the roux becomes the color of fudge. This may take about fifteen minutes, but don't stop stirring to do anything else. Rouxs are easy to burn. If you burn your roux, throw it out and start over or you will ruin your recipe! It is better to have your roux undercooked than burned.

How to Make Pan Gravy

Pan gravy is made in the same pan in which meat has been cooked, and it uses the juices and flavors from the meat to season the gravy. First, remove the cooked meat from the pan and set it aside to cool. Pour all the liquid from the pan into a large measuring cup. Almost immediately the fat will start to float to the top of the cup, leaving the good juice on the bottom. If it looks as though there's a lot of fat, you can add a few ice cubes to the measuring cup. Ice cubes will attract the grease; in a minute or two you can spoon out the greasy ice cubes and throw them away. In any case, you'll want to remove as much fat as you can from the cup before you make the gravy.

While the fat is rising to the top, scrape the pan to loosen the pieces of meat. You'll need those scraps for the gravy. Then take ¼ cup flour and put it in a jar with about 1½ cups of meat juice. (If you don't have enough meat juice, supplement it with *cold* water.) Put the lid on the jar and shake like crazy until the flour is evenly mixed with the liquid. Try not to leave any lumps, or you'll have lumpy gravy. Set the jar aside and finish scooping the fat out of the cup of drippings. Throw the fat away and pour the drippings and the flour mixture into the pan. Stir over medium-high heat until the mixture reaches gravy consistency. Add salt and pepper to taste. Serve immediately. This recipe makes about 2 cups gravy. If you want to make more gravy, add more flour and meat juice or *cold* water in the same proportions that you used for the original 2-cup yield.

How to Mince Garlic

You can purchase crushed or chopped garlic from the store, but it doesn't taste the same as fresh minced garlic. Fresh garlic is purchased in bulbs, and each bulb can be opened to reveal multiple sections called cloves. Many recipes call for minced garlic, which is a term for garlic that has been chopped extremely fine.

Start by opening the garlic bulb and removing the cloves. Each clove is covered with a paper-like skin that must be removed. Cut away the woody area where the clove was attached to the bulb. This should free up the white skin so that it can be peeled off with a knife. Sometimes hitting each clove with the flat side of a large knife blade will also loosen the skin so that it can be removed.

Now that you have the peeled cloves, you are ready to mince the garlic. If you do this a lot, you might want to invest in a garlic press, which presses the cloves through a series of small holes, turning it to paste. If you don't have a press, use the knife to dice all of the cloves, cutting them first one way and then the other, until you have a pile of small garlic pieces. Gather the diced pieces and chop them by moving the knife from back to front in a rocking motion. One portion of the knife should always be touching the cutting board as you rock it back and forth from front to back. Pause to gather the garlic back into a pile and to remove any sticking to the side of the knife. Continue until the garlic is in very, very fine pieces.

How to Mix Ingredients for Baking

The order in which you mix ingredients for baking is important. If you put the dry ingredients in the bowl first, you will end up with pockets of dry ingredients in your batter that will never mix in with the other ingredients. *Always* mix the dry and wet ingredients separately first. Then add the wet ingredients into the bigger bowl and then slowly add the dry ingredients to the bowl. That way you're more likely to have a batter where all the ingredients are properly mixed.

How to Prepare Chicken Wings

These days, so many people are cooking chicken wings that it's possible to get them already cut apart in your supermarket freezer case. But just in case your grocer doesn't carry them, it's easy enough to buy whole chicken wings and prepare them yourself. Using a chopping board and a sharp knife, cut each wing at the joints to make three sections—a "drumstick" with one bone, a piece with two bones, and the wing tip. Throw the wing tip away; the other two pieces are the pieces you'll use. If a recipe calls for three pounds of chicken wings, you'll want to buy three and a half pounds to make up for the parts you'll be throwing away.

How to Prepare a Turkey for Cooking

A good rule of thumb for buying a turkey is to allow 2 pounds of meat for every person you plan to serve. When in doubt, buy a larger turkey and enjoy the leftovers. The hardest part about cooking a turkey is getting ready to cook it. First, you need to find a pan that's big enough for your bird. Turkeys are traditionally cooked in roasting pans, but many ovens are not large enough to accommodate roasting pans (or even large turkeys). If your oven isn't big enough for the turkey, there's nothing you can do about it; but if it's just not big enough for a roasting pan you can get a pan made of crinkled aluminum foil for a few dollars in the grocery store. These can be bent to fit around the turkey and inside the oven.

Once you have your pan, you need to make sure your turkey is completely thawed. Allow at least three days to thaw your turkey, still in the wrapper, in your refrigerator. Or you can save yourself the trouble and buy a turkey that has never been frozen. After your turkey is completely thawed, you can remove the plastic wrapper. Do it in the (clean!) kitchen sink, so you don't get juice everywhere.

There are two cavities in the bird—one in the neck area, and one under the tail. Make sure to remove any bagged organ meat (gizzard, heart, liver, and neck) from those cavities. You can cook them and eat them, feed them to your pets, or just throw them away. There is also a neck you'll want to remove, but don't ever feed poultry bones to animals. When these items are removed, you are ready to cook the turkey.

Preheat the oven to 325 degrees. Once the turkey is completely thawed, remove it from the wrapper and get rid of the bagged organ meats and the neck. Pat the outside of the turkey dry with paper towels and then cover the outside skin with cooking oil or cooking spray. Pour about ½ cup water in the bottom of a large roasting pan. Place the turkey breast side up in the pan. Place aluminum foil loosely over the top to prevent the top from burning. Place roasting pan in the oven. If the turkey doesn't have a built-in timer, cook until the juices run clear when you stab it with a fork, or until the wings move easily apart from the body when you pull on them. Most turkeys have a timer that will pop out when the turkey is cooked. Take the turkey out of the oven and let it cool for 30 minutes before carving. Save the juice for making gravy.

Here are approximate cooking times, based on turkey weight:

8 to 12 pounds	2¾ to 3 hours
12 to 14 pounds	3 to 3¾ hours
14 to 18 pounds	3¾ to 4¼ hours
18 to 20 pounds	4¼ to 4½ hours
20 to 24 pounds	4½ to 5 hours

What Kind of Baking Dishes Should I Buy?

If you're looking for a reliable pan for single-layer cakes or brownies, you can't go wrong with a glass baking dish. They come in two shapes—square (great for brownies) or rectangular (most rectangular pans are 9x13-inches and are the perfect size for one-layer cakes). Glass baking dishes are good because cakes and brownies don't stick to them (especially if you spray the insides with cooking spray or rub them with butter or oil before adding your ingredients). This makes them easier to clean. Bowl-shaped glass dishes (or any glass dish with deep sides) are called casserole dishes and are used in many of the recipes in this book.

Appendix B
Cooking Terms and Ingredients

Nothing is more frustrating than reading through a delicious new recipe and discover some ingredient or kitchen tool that is completely alien to you. We've tried to ease that frustration in this section, by defining many of the terms found in this book that may not be familiar, particularly to new cooks. These are generally the names of ingredients, cooking tools, or common cooking procedures.

Allspice—A powdered spice that is said to combine the flavors of cinnamon, nutmeg, and cloves. You can find it in the spice aisle of the market.

Anchovies—A small fish usually preserved in oil and salt, often used in salads, spreads, and dips. Look in the canned seafood or international sections of the market.

Artichoke Hearts—the inside of the artichoke, under the leaves. Usually they are marinated in oil for use in salads and other recipes.

Baguette—A long, stiff loaf of French bread that is crusty on the outside and soft on the inside.

Bake—To cook in an oven with the oven door closed; usually applies to baked goods such as cookies or cakes.

Baking Dish—Any dish that can be safely used inside an oven. Glass baking dishes are ideal because food doesn't stick to them as easily as it does to metal baking dishes.

Baking Powder—A leavening agent used in cakes and cookies to make them rise. It is often sold in a round can with a plastic lid.

Baking Soda—Similar to baking powder, but it can also be used in candies. Baking powder and baking soda are *not* interchangeable in recipes! Baking soda is usually sold in a box.

Basil—A leaf that is used fresh in salads or dried as a seasoning. Fresh basil is found in the produce section; dried basil leaves are found in the spice section.

Baste—Spoon juices from cooking or leftover marinade over meat during the cooking process. This keeps the meat moist.

Bay Leaf—A leaf that is used as flavoring for soups and stews. Look for it in the spice section of the supermarket.

Beat—To mix ingredients with a fork, wire whisk, or electric mixer so that all the ingredients are smooth and ready to bake or serve.

Black Pepper—The stuff that comes out of the pepper shaker.

Boil—Heat a liquid until bubbles come up to the top. Water boils at 212 degrees Fahrenheit at sea level.

Bread Crumbs—You can make them yourself by rubbing bread between your hands, or you can buy them already seasoned and crunchy in the bread aisle or baking supplies aisle of the supermarket.

Broil—To cook with heat coming from above. If you broil in an oven, it isn't broiling unless the oven door is open. If the door is closed, you're "roasting."

Broiler—Any cooking appliance that can broil. This could be a separate broiler, an oven, or a toaster oven.

Broiler Pan—A two-part pan used for broiling. The bottom part is a solid pan to catch dripping liquids. The top is a piece with holes that you can put meat on. As the meat cooks, the grease drips down to the lower part of the pan, away from the food.

Broth—A liquid that results when you boil meat or vegetables in water.

Buffalo Wings—Spicy appetizers that come from a chicken, not a bison. They were invented in Buffalo, New York (hence the name), and are usually served with celery sticks and bleu cheese dressing.

Butter—Something that is NOT replaceable with margarine in any of our recipes! Replacing the butter can affect the outcome of the recipe, not to mention the food won't taste as good.

Cake Mix—A mixture of flour, sugar, flavorings, and leavening agents that many people use to make their "homemade" cakes.

Cake Pan—Any pan of whatever shape or material that is used to bake a cake.

Capers—Buds from a tree, packed in brine. They taste like small green olives, and are usually found with the olives and pickles in the market.

Casserole Dish—This is an oven-proof cooking dish designed for casseroles. It is similar to a baking dish, but is deeper.

Cayenne Pepper—Also referred to as "red" pepper, it is much hotter than black pepper.

Celery Salt—A seasoning blend made with ground celery seeds and salt.

Cheddar Cheese—A hard cheese, usually yellow, that is used in many American dishes.

Chicken Breast—The largest piece of meat on the chicken, it is considered "white" meat.

Chicken Broth—A liquid made by cooking chicken in salted water, it is usually used in soups, gravies, and stews.

Chicken Wings—The part of the chicken that flapped. Chicken wings come in three pieces: a "drumstick," a center section, and the pointed wing tip. All but the wing tips are used to make buffalo wings and other chicken wing dishes.

Chili Oil—Orange-colored oil used in Oriental cooking to add spice to a dish. You can find it in the international or Oriental foods section of the market.

Chili Powder—A reddish-colored ground spice that is often used in chili and similar dishes. It is made from ground red chili peppers and is not as spicy as cayenne pepper. It can be found in the spice section of the market.

Chop—To cut into small pieces (about the size of a fingernail).

Cilantro—Also known as "Chinese parsley" and "Mexican parsley," it is a staple of Mexican and Asian cooking. Look for it in the produce section of your supermarket. You can also find it in the spice section as "coriander," but it doesn't taste at all the same when it's ground and dried.

Colander—Also known as a strainer, it is used to drain liquid off pasta and other foods.

Condensed Milk—Also called "sweetened condensed milk," but the word "sweetened" isn't needed because there is no condensed milk that isn't sweet. This is milk that comes in cans and is used for cooking desserts. Find it in the baking aisle of the supermarket. Don't confuse it with evaporated milk, which is thinner and not nearly as sweet.

Cookie Sheet—A flat metal sheet that is used to bake cookies.

Cooking Spray—A spray product that is used to "grease" baking pans or cookie sheets. The spray comes in various flavors. You may not want to use garlic-flavored spray or even olive oil spray if you're making cookies.

Cornstarch—A multi-purpose item used in baby powders as well as to thicken gravies and sauces.

Cornmeal—Ground dried corn; it is used to make corn tortillas, cornbread, and other delights. It is often sprinkled on pizza pans to keep the pizza from sticking to the pan.

Crab Boil—A mix of pungent seasonings, sold in a box. It is also sold in liquid form, but those are nasty chemicals that should be avoided. Sniff the box before you buy. If it doesn't make you sneeze, it's not fresh and you may want to use two bags instead of one.

Cream—What floats to the top after a cow has been milked.

Craisins®—Ocean Spray's version of dried, sweetened cranberries, used in recipes as you'd use raisins. Find them near the raisins in the supermarket.

Cream Cheese—A smooth and spreadable cheese used for dips and cooking. It usually comes in the form of white bricks that are wrapped in foil and sold in boxes in the dairy case.

Curry Powder—A strong spice often used in Indian cooking. Look for it in the spice section.

Cutting Board—A surface that is used to protect the counter or table when you are chopping or cutting ingredients for cooking. Do not use wooden cutting boards for cutting meat, because bacteria could get down in the wood and give you food poisoning later.

Dash—A sprinkle of a spice. Usually a dash is officially measured as ⅛ teaspoon.

Deep Fry—To cook over direct heat in oil that covers the item being cooked. If the oil is shallow, it is called "pan frying."

Deveined Shrimp—Some shrimp have a dark vein running down the back that makes the shrimp taste gritty. If you can't find shrimp where these have been removed (deveined), you may have to do this yourself using a knife or pick.

Dice—To chop in small pieces. If "chopping" produces fingernail-sized pieces, dicing produces pieces that are half that size.

Diced Tomatoes—Tomatoes that have been diced. They are usually sold in cans, and you can get them with various spices or flavors to enhance your cooking.

Dijon Mustard—A medium-hot mustard that originated in France.

Dollop—A blob of something. You can put a dollop of whipped cream on your shortcake, for example. Dollops can be as big or small as you want. You don't need to measure a blob.

Egg Noodles—Noodles that are made with egg yolks. They look and taste just like other noodles, so buy the noodles that are cheapest and that are shaped the way you want.

Evaporated Milk—Canned milk that tastes like milk with some of the water taken out. This is not to be confused with condensed milk, which is sinfully sweet.

Fennel Seeds—Seeds that have a licorice taste. If a recipe calls for them, don't leave them out! Buy them in the spice section of the supermarket.

Feta Cheese—A cheese that has curds rather than being solid, and that is usually made with the milk of goats or sheep.

Field Greens—A gourmet mixture of salad greens, which have different textures and tastes.

Fold—Gently combining liquid ingredients by turning one part over the other with a rubber bowl scraper. Ingredients are folded together when they would be harmed by harsher mixing techniques.

Fry—Cook over direct heat in oil.

Frying Pan—Also known as a skillet, a wide and shallow pan that is used for frying.

Garlic—Sold in "bulbs," garlic is found in the produce section of the supermarket. An individual piece of garlic in the bulb is called a "clove" of garlic.

Garlic Powder—Garlic that has been dried and ground to use as a seasoning. Look for it in the spice section of the supermarket.

Garlic Press—A handy gadget with tiny holes that is used to squeeze garlic cloves into tiny strands for cooking.

Garlic Salt—Powdered garlic that has been combined with salt to use as a seasoning.

Ginger—A pungent spice that is sold ground (in the spice section) or as a root (in the produce section).

Grated Cheese—Cheese that has been put through a cheese grater to shred it into small pieces. You can grate cheese yourself or buy it already grated in the dairy case.

Green Chilies—Usually refers to diced, mild chili peppers that are sold in small cans in the Mexican foods section of the supermarket.

Green Onions—Sold in the produce section of the supermarket, they are long plants with a white bottom and long green tops. Both the white and the green parts can be eaten, but be sure to wash them well first.

Half-and-Half—A mixture of equal parts cream and milk.

Heavy Cream—Cream that has a higher percentage of butterfat than regular cream.

Hot Oil—*See* Chili Oil.

Italian Seasoning—A blend of spices that are used in Italian cooking, most notably basil and oregano. Look for it in the spice section of the supermarket.

Jalapeño Peppers—Spicy peppers often used in Mexican foods that also add zing to nachos and tuna fish sandwiches. Peppers are usually sliced or diced, packed into bottles, and found in the Mexican foods section of the market.

Kitchen Shears—This is a special kind of heavy-duty scissor designed for kitchen tasks, such as cutting meat. Buy a good brand at a kitchen supply store, and resist the urge to use them for other cutting chores. Be sure to wash and dry them between uses!

Lemon Juice—When a recipe calls for lemon juice, you can buy a container of it in the freezer section of the market. You will also find unrefrigerated varieties in the produce or juice sections, but these generally are not as good. Or, you can always make your own by squeezing a lemon. There is even a handy kitchen gadget (lemon juicer) that will help do this.

Margarine—A nasty butter substitute that we hope you're not using in any of our recipes. If you must use margarine in cooking, use it only in sticks. The stuff in tubs has a lot of water and air added, and will ruin whatever recipe you're cooking.

Marinade—A liquid used to marinate food in cooking.

Marinate—The act of soaking meat or other food in a savory liquid as a way to flavor the food.

Mandarin Oranges—Sold in cans, mandarin oranges look and taste like peeled tangerine sections.

Mince—To chop in the tiniest pieces imaginable.

Nutmeg—A spice that is grated and used in baking. You can grate your own with a nutmeg grater, but most people buy it pre-grated in the spice section of the supermarket.

Orange Oil—Oil that is made from the peel of the orange. It is used in frosting and salad dressings. Buy it in the gourmet section (or the spice section) of your supermarket.

Orange Zest—This is a fancy word for grated orange peels. You can buy it in the spice aisle of the market, or make your own with a grater and an orange peel. If you make your own, be sure to grate only the colored peel; the white part is bitter.

Oregano—A leaf used for seasoning. Buy it dried in the spice aisle, or as fresh leaves in the produce section of better markets.

Paprika—A red spice that is used to add color as well as flavor to foods.

Parsley Flakes—This spice is made from dehydrated and chopped parsley and can be found on the spice aisle of your market.

Picanté Sauce—Picanté is Spanish for spicy. Look for jars of this sauce in the Mexican foods section of the supermarket.

Pickle Relish—A condiment made from chopped pickles that is often used on hamburgers and hot dogs. You can find sweet and dill varieties, usually near the ketchup.

Pie Filling—Cans of sweetened fruit (cherries, blueberries, apples) in a thickened juice, which is used in fruit pies and other pastries. Look for it with the baking ingredients.

Pinto Beans—Brown beans that are used for refried beans and in other recipes. You can find them dried with the other beans in the supermarket, or canned with the rest of the canned beans.

Pita Bread—Bread that is used in the Middle East in much the same way as tortillas are used in Mexico. The differences are that pita bread is always made from flour, rather than from cornmeal, and that it is thicker than your basic tortilla. It is also hollow, so if you cut it in half you can fill it.

Popover—A little puff of bread that usually has a hollow center. Popovers can be filled with ham salad or some other mixture and then eaten as appetizers, but more often they're eaten with meat and gravy.

Poultry Seasoning—Any seasoning used to enhance poultry. The main ingredient of poultry seasoning found in the spice section of the supermarket is sage.

Red Pepper Flakes—Hot seeds from red chili peppers, usually shaken on foods or into soups to add flavor.

Rice Vinegar—Vinegar made from rice. There are both seasoned and unseasoned varieties, and both are found in the Oriental foods section of the supermarket.

Roast—To cook meat uncovered in an oven.

Rosemary—Needles from the rosemary bush. They add seasoning to poultry and other dishes. You can get fresh rosemary twigs in the produce section or buy it dried in the spice aisle.

Roux—A mixture of flour and some kind of oil, which is used to thicken soups and sauces and stews.

Rubber Bowl Scraper—A flat, pliable piece of rubber or silicone on a stick. Often referred to as "spatulas" or "rubber spatulas," these tools do just what the name implies.

Sage—An herb that is used for seasoning. It is usually rubbed into a powdery substance, and is often referred to as "rubbed sage." Look for it on the spice aisle.

Salad Dressing—There are two definitions for salad dressing. As used in recipes, "salad dressing" is usually the mayonnaise-like stuff that is sweet. (Miracle Whip is salad dressing.) The other definition is the one you already know, which is the stuff you pour on a salad that turns it into a salad.

Salsa—A mixture of tomatoes, onions, vegetables, and cilantro that is used as a condiment for Mexican foods.

Saucepan—As the name implies, this is a small- to medium-sized pan usually used for trivial cooking tasks such as making sauces. Buy several at the cooking supply store.

Sauté—To cook over low to medium heat in a small amount of fat. If what you're cooking is vegetables, you cook them until they are no longer crunchy.

Seasoning Salt—Any mixture of salt and other seasonings used to enhance food. Although there are hundreds of varieties on the market, Jane's Krazy Mixed-Up Salt® is one of our favorites.

Sesame Oil—Oil made from crushed sesame seeds, it is used to impart flavor to salad dressings and other recipes.

Shredded Cheese—*See* Grated Cheese.

Sifted Flour—Flour that has been put through a sifter. Sifting adds volume to flour, so if a recipe calls for sifted flour, it will take less flour than if the flour weren't sifted first.

Simmer—To cook a liquid just below the boiling point.

Skillet—A frying pan.

Sour Cream—Cream that has fermented. Look for it in the dairy case of the supermarket.

Spatula—This tool is used to manipulate foods while cooking, such as flipping pancakes and removing cookies from a warm cookie sheet. True spatulas are hard; rubber ones used to scrape the side of bowls are properly called "rubber bowl scrapers."

Steam—To cook with steam. Usually this is done in a "steamer" that holds food in a holey container that sits above boiling water.

Stew Beef—Beef that has been cubed and trimmed for stew. It is sold in packages at the meat counter.

Stewed Tomatoes—Tomatoes that have been peeled and cooked, often with other vegetables such as celery and onions.

Sweet Onions—Sweet onions look like regular onions, but they are labeled "sweet onions" in the supermarket. They aren't as strong as regular white or yellow onions and have a much more agreeable flavor.

Teriyaki Sauce—A sweet sauce used in Japanese cooking, found in the Oriental foods section of the market.

Tomato Paste—A thick paste made by cooking down tomatoes until much of the water is removed. It is sold with the canned tomatoes in the supermarket.

Tomato Sauce—Similar to tomato paste, but with not as much water cooked out.

Tortillas—Round, flat bread made of cornmeal or flour, used in Mexican cuisine.

Vanilla—A flavoring made with vanilla beans. Look for it in bottles on the spice aisle, and do not be tempted to buy the cheaper chemical substitute, vanillin.

Vegetable Oil—Cooking oil made of any one of a number of vegetables, grains, or even fruits. Corn oil is a popular example.

Vegetable Scrubber—This is a brush-like tool that is used to clean vegetables and fruits prior to using. Do not use them for other cleaning tasks, such as scrubbing pots.

Whipping Cream—A light cream that is used to make whipped cream, but that is also used without whipping in other recipes. Look for it with the milk in your grocer's dairy case.

White Cheese—Any one of a number of cheeses (such as Parmesan, mozzarella, Swiss, or Monterey Jack) that are white rather than yellow.

Wire Whisk—A wire cage on a stick, used for whipping egg yolks or other ingredients.

Worcestershire Sauce—A brown condiment that comes from England. Look for it with the ketchups and barbecue sauces.

Zest—Grated rind from a citrus fruit. You can make your own, or buy it in the spice aisle of the supermarket. Homemade is fresher, but it's a pain in the neck to make!

Appendix C
Basic Cooking Equipment

Here is a list of everything you'll need to make every recipe that is included in this book. We're assuming you already have an oven and a cooking top; other than those two things, these are the supplies you'll want:

Mixing bowls

Measuring spoons

Measuring cups

2-quart saucepan (with lid)

One large pot (with lid)

One 8x8-inch glass baking dish

One or two 9x13-inch glass baking dishes

One glass casserole dish (a big square or round dish with a lid)

One frying pan

One rubber bowl scraper (also referred to as a rubber spatula; it is used for mixing)

One metal or plastic spatula (it is used for lifting things from a pan or cookie sheet)

One large cooking spoon (metal or plastic)

One large slotted cooking spoon (metal or plastic, used to remove solids and leave the liquids behind)

One cookie sheet

One colander (you may know it as a strainer, to get the water out of your spaghetti)

Electric mixer (optional, but it makes things easier)

Four Seasoning Blends to Customize Your Recipes

Occasionally a recipe will call for seasoning salt. Even if recipes don't call for seasoning salt, you may find you want to spice up your recipes with a seasoning blend. Here are the best we've found in about a million years of cooking. One is the best all-purpose seasoning salt on the planet; the others are for chicken, for beef, and for seafood—and they're all available in any of the larger supermarket chains:

Jane's Krazy Mixed-Up Salt®

Chef Paul Prudhomme's Magic Seasoning Blends—Poultry Magic®

McCormick Grill Mates®—Montreal Steak Seasoning

Chef Paul Prudhomme's Magic Seasoning Blends—Seafood Magic®

Index